GUIDEPOSTS
for Veterinary
Professionals

Guideposts for Veterinary Professionals is published by
the American Veterinary Medical History Society as
a service to the veterinary medical profession.

Citation: Aiello SE, Currier RW, eds. *Guideposts for Veterinary Professionals*. The American Veterinary Medical History Society; 2021.

ISBN: 978-1-7368471-0-7

Published by the American Veterinary Medical History Society
in partnership with *The Merck Veterinary Manual*.

 MERCKVETMANUAL.COM

Design by Sheryl Lazenby of SmartDog Design, Pickerington, Ohio
Printed by Sheridan, Chelsea, Michigan

About the AVMHS

Founded in 1978, the American Veterinary Medical History Society, Inc. (AVMHS) is dedicated to the education, research, and service in the field of veterinary medical history. Its primary objectives are to promote research and writing on veterinary history, to communicate such information through its publications and meetings, and to serve as a resource for information about veterinary history.

Activities and membership benefits include the following:

- *Veterinary Heritage* (AVMHS journal, published twice a year)
- *Interim News & Comment* (periodic newsletter)
- Essay contest for veterinary students with cash prizes
- Registry of Heritage Veterinary Practices (practices that have been in continuous operation for more than 50 years)
- Annual meeting, supplemented by occasional regional meetings and/or special presentations
- Opportunities to serve on the AVMHS Board or various committees and to network with others interested in veterinary history

Additional activities focus on veterinary museums, vintage medical instruments, book collecting, oral history interviews, short historical articles called *Time-Bites*, postcards for annual meetings, and more.

Anyone interested in the history of veterinary medicine is welcome to join the AVMHS. For more information, please visit https://www.avmhs.org

The AVMHS is a 501(c)3 nonprofit educational organization.

GUIDEPOSTS
for Veterinary Professionals

Editors
Susan E. Aiello, DVM, ELS
Russell W. Currier, DVM, MPH, DACVPM

Editorial Board
Margaret N. Carter, DVM, MS, MSS, DACVPM
Howard H. Erickson, DVM, PhD
Jerry M. Owens, DVM, DACVR
Susanne K. Whitaker, MSLS, AHIP
Zbigniew W. Wojcinski, DVM, DVSc, DACVP, DABT, FIATP

CONTENTS

Preface

The idea for this handbook was conceived in Pittsburgh in May 2018, while I was attending the 48th annual meeting of the American Osler Society, an organization dedicated to preserving the memory of Sir William Osler and to promoting the study of medical history and related humanities. At this meeting, I presented a paper describing the 20th-century research and work of veterinarian Karl F. Meyer and physician Richard Shope (often mistaken for being a veterinarian) and drew parallels to the life and career of Sir William Osler.

As is the case at most meetings, a limited assortment of publications was available for purchase, including a small just-published handbook entitled *Osler for White Coat Pockets*, by Drs. Joseph B. VanderVeer and Charles S. Bryan, intended for distribution to medical students at the time of their white coat ceremonies. This little book of approximately 175 pages was replete with Osler's wisdom and approach to medicine's challenges and how best to deal with them, including a great deal on integrating a happy and meaningful life in and out of a career in medicine.

On my flight home, I read more than half of this small book and, needless to say, I was impressed. I saw an opportunity for a comparable publication for the veterinary student community that would include emphasis on Osler, along with content of specific and direct relevance to veterinary medicine. Others in the AVMHS agreed that this would be a worthwhile project, and so we began.

We hope you find the content useful not only in your student days but also in the years afterward. A veterinary education is daunting. Packing in all that knowledge and embarking on your professional career can be overwhelming on many an occasion, and I trust that *Guideposts* may provide an occasional break and encouragement.

Guideposts for Veterinary Professionals comprises various topics to offer guidance for effectively dealing with the challenges of your education and subsequent career in the veterinary medical profession. In addition to reflecting the historical wisdom of Sir William Osler in human medicine, *Guideposts* reflects the additional challenge within the veterinary profession of dealing with both the patient and the client.

Osler (1849–1919)—with a career that extended from the last quarter of the 19th century through most of the first quarter of the 20th century—is a revered figure in human medicine that extends to today. Veterinarians can also claim Osler as one of their own. He taught veterinary students at McGill, served as president of a veterinary association in Canada, and conducted numerous investigations into animal diseases, discovering the dog lungworm presently named *Oslerus osleri.*

Russell W. Currier, DVM, MPH, DACVPM

Foreword

Guideposts for Veterinary Professionals was conceived and written to serve the profession as an inspirational and portable "life coach." Throughout any veterinary education and career, there will be challenges when a trusted resource can provide a refuge during times of doubt. This handbook can guide you during those challenging times, providing not only useful advice and perspective but also set out aspirational goals for your career and life.

The topics of this handbook were chosen for their breadth and professional relevance. Historical precedent is highlighted throughout to illustrate the challenges and perspectives of veterinarians of the past in order to serve and guide the veterinarians of younger generations. The professional and life experiences of *Guideposts'* authors can provide sage advice for 21st-century veterinarians. The authors use vignettes and historical quotes to highlight various approaches and solutions. Client interactions and expectations are featured as a source of both great challenge and great reward. The examples cited in this handbook stand the test of time for all generations of veterinarians.

An important concept for the veterinary medical profession is that of work-life balance. The reward that comes from engaging with our work on the job with energy and enthusiasm must be properly balanced with the benefit we reap when we disengage from our careers for our families, other personal connections, and non-work activities. Consulting this handbook frequently can serve as a source of professional perspective and inspiration, as well as a reminder to maintain our personal well-being and a balanced life. Reading a chapter each night may allow reflection on the day that has past and help focus our energies and passion for the days ahead.

Trevor R. Ames, DVM, MS, DACVIM

INTRODUCTION

Welcome to the inaugural edition of *Guideposts for Veterinary Professionals!* Our hope is that within these pages you will find sound and succinct advice on your veterinary education, the development of your career, professionalism, and a balanced life. Although *Guideposts* was developed for veterinary students and recent graduates, we believe that veterinarians of all ages will find some beneficial counsel.

The major sections of *Guideposts* consider our shared mission and service as veterinarians, a veterinary education and career choices, and a focus on relationships with our patients, clients, colleagues, and mentors. Also included is the significant role of veterinarians in the welfare of all animal species and in the human-animal bond, as well as sage and practical advice on self-care while dealing with the many stressors of practice. Other concepts include recognizing the importance of keen observation, which may offer much more toward a diagnosis than myriad laboratory tests, and remembering that practicing medicine, problem solving, and learning skill sets takes time.

A special chapter is dedicated to the life, work, and great wisdom of Sir William Osler, a legendary physician from the late 19th and early 20th century. Dr. Osler was a man for all medicine, contributing significantly not only to human medicine but also to comparative and veterinary medicine. Osler was a prolific writer, and his teachings are timeless in their wisdom, as relevant today as when they were written over a century ago. Integrating these philosophies into your thinking will increase your effectiveness in all aspects of life by helping you to consistently exhibit good character, take an ethical approach to problem solving, and develop confidence to guide your actions.

Guideposts also aims to demonstrate the value of embracing the rich history of the veterinary medical profession and the humanities, and we encourage you to add books focused on medical and veterinary history to your personal reference library. The study of history can provide solace during difficult times, knowing that those before you have also been tested by problematic experiences.

As times change more and more rapidly, we must adapt and be flexible in our careers and our lives. Fortunately, your veterinary education has prepared you for a variety of career options and trajectories, and the demand for veterinarians continues to increase. Commit to lifelong learning, and you will find that your chosen profession will offer new opportunities.

We are deeply grateful to our contributing authors, all leaders in the veterinary medical profession who willingly shared their insights, perspectives, and personal experiences. We also wish to acknowledge our partnership with *The Merck Veterinary Manual,* which has provided financial support to print *Guideposts,* as well as access to content for all students on the *Merck Manuals Student Stories* site (https://vetstudentstories.merckmanuals.com/).

Finally, we welcome your feedback and suggestions for how we may improve *Guideposts* for the new generations of veterinarians in the years ahead.

Susan E. Aiello, DVM, ELS
Russell W. Currier, DVM, MPH, DACVPM

CONTRIBUTING AUTHORS

Dana G. Allen, DVM, MSc, DACVIM
Professor Emeritus, Ontario Veterinary College
University of Guelph, Canada
Assessment, Diagnosis, and Therapeutic Plan

Trevor R. Ames, DVM, MS, DACVIM
Associate Vice President of Academic Health Sciences and
Professor of Veterinary Medicine, University of Minnesota
Science and Art in Veterinary Medicine

Danelle Bickett-Weddle, DVM, MPH, PhD, DACVPM
Past President
American College of Veterinary Preventive Medicine
Specialization

Michael J. Blackwell, DVM, MPH, FNAP
Former Dean, College of Veterinary Medicine
University of Tennessee
The Golden Rule and Ethics

Lawrence A. Busch, DVM, MDiv
Love and Service

Craig N. Carter, DVM, MS, PhD, DACVPM, DSNAP
Director and Professor, Veterinary Diagnostic Laboratory
University of Kentucky
Mentors and Mentoring

Heather Case, DVM, MPH, DACVPM, CAE
Chief Executive Officer
International Council for Veterinary Assessment
Career Progression and Change

Michael Chaddock, DVM, EML
Diversity and Demographics

Susan P. Cohen, DSW
Founder, Pet Decisions
Balance and Reflection

Kathleen Cooney, DVM, CHPV, CCFP
Director of Education
Companion Animal Euthanasia Training Academy
Client Counseling, Comfort Care, and Euthanasia

Russell W. Currier, DVM, MPH, DACVPM
Past President
American Veterinary Medical History Society
Relationship Skills
Competency and Caring

W. Ron DeHaven, DVM, MBA
Former Administrator, US Department of Agriculture
Animal & Plant Health Inspection Service
The Importance of Character

Michael Dicks, PhD
Chief Data Human, Erupt, LLC
Driving Forces in the Veterinary Profession

Howard H. Erickson, DVM, PhD
Professor Emeritus, College of Veterinary Medicine
Kansas State University
Luminaries in Veterinary Medicine

Ken Gorczyca, DVM
Founder, Lesbian and Gay Veterinary Medical Association
Diversity and Demographics

Eleanor M. Green, DVM, DACVIM, DABVP
Senior Advisor & Consultant, Animal Policy Group
Dean Emeritus, College of Veterinary Medicine &
Biomedical Sciences, Texas A&M University
Generational Change

Daniel L. Grooms, DVM, PhD, DACVM
Stephen G. Juelsgaard Dean, College of Veterinary Medicine
Iowa State University
Integrity, Honesty, Humility, and Kindness

Marie Holowaychuk, DVM, DACVECC, CYT
Small Animal ECC Specialist and Wellbeing Advocate
Self-Care

John Herbold, DVM, MPH, PhD, DACVPM, DACAW, FACE, FNAP
UTHealth School of Public Health, The University of Texas
Knowledge and Wisdom

COL (Ret) Jerry Jaax, DVM, DACLAM
Former Associate Vice President for Research Compliance
Kansas State University
Scientific and Moral Courage and Fortitude

COL (Ret) Nancy Jaax, DVM, DACVP
Special Projects Officer, Office of Sponsored Research Programs
Kansas State University
Scientific and Moral Courage and Fortitude

Candace A. Jacobs, DVM, MPH, DACVPM, CFS
Versatile Profession

Lonnie J. King, DVM, MS, MPA, DACVPM
Academy Professor and Dean Emeritus
College of Veterinary Medicine, The Ohio State University
Professionalism and Professional Identity
Veterinary College

Melissa Maddux, DVM
CEO, Erupt, LLC
Driving Forces in the Veterinary Profession

Roger K. Mahr, DVM
Past President, American Veterinary Medical Association
Organized Veterinary Medicine and Collaborative Leadership

Sara Mark, DVM
President and Chief Medical Officer
Southwest Veterinary Hospital, PC
The Human-Animal Bond

Donald L. Noah, DVM, MPH, DACVPM
Assistant Dean for One Health and
Executive Director for Animal and Human Health in Appalachia
Lincoln Memorial University Colleges of Veterinary
Medicine and Osteopathic Medicine
Our Mission
Confidence, Trust, Hope, and Optimism

Jerry M. Owens, DVM, DACVR
Veterinary Radiology Consultant
Private Practice

Abbie Viscardi, PhD
Research Assistant Professor
College of Veterinary Medicine, Kansas State University
Animal Welfare

Lorin D. Warnick, DVM, PhD, DACVPM
Austin O. Hooey Dean of Veterinary Medicine
Cornell University College of Veterinary Medicine
Fairness and Social Responsibility

Zbigniew W. Wojcinski, DVM, DVSc, DACVP, DABT, FIATP
President, Toxicology & Pathology Consulting, LLC
Sir William Osler: The Significance of His Life to Veterinary Medicine

"Do the right thing and do it first."

–Sir William Osler, MD

SIR WILLIAM OSLER

SIR WILLIAM OSLER: THE SIGNIFICANCE OF HIS LIFE TO VETERINARY MEDICINE

Zbigniew W. Wojcinski, DVM, DVSc, DACVP, DABT, FIATP

Reproduced by permission of the Osler Library of the History of Medicine, McGill University.

Sir William Osler is well known worldwide in the medical community as an extraordinary physician. But he was more than that. His influence extended to other disciplines, including veterinary medicine. Osler pioneered the idea of comparative pathology and made fundamental contributions to veterinary education. As veterinarians, we can benefit enormously from understanding how William Osler integrated science with medicine and humanity to the benefit of all.

Early Years and Education

William Osler was born on July 12, 1849, in Bond Head, Ontario, Canada, to parents of Celtic origin and was one of nine children. As a child, he was mischievous and a practical joker—traits that often landed him in trouble in his youth but stayed with him throughout his career. William was an excellent student and attended a private boarding school in Weston, Ontario, where he came under the tutelage of the school's warden, Reverend W.A. Johnson. Both a naturalist and biologist, Rev. Johnson was, at that time, one of the few individuals in Canada capable of mounting and examining microscopic preparations. He introduced young William to the microscope and, together, they collected numerous specimens, which they mounted on slides for further study.

William entered Trinity College at the University of Toronto in 1867. Under the influence and encouragement of Dr. James Bovell, a physician and naturalist who was professor of pathology and physiology at the Toronto School of Medicine and also a lecturer in parasitology at the Ontario Veterinary College, Osler pursued the study of internal parasites and trichinosis in particular—his introduction to veterinary medicine.

Osler studied medicine at the Toronto School of Medicine for 2 years and then transferred to McGill Medical College in Montreal for another 2 years, receiving his Doctor of Medicine (with distinction) in 1872 at the age of 23. He then pursued informal postgraduate education for 2 years in western Europe, which was considered the center of medical science at the time. He went first to London to study histology and physiology, then to Berlin to study pathology with the German physician Rudolf Virchow, and later to Leipzig and Vienna. Virchow kindled Osler's interest in pathology, which remained with him until the end of his career. Osler admired Virchow's teaching methods, particularly his use of the microscope in lectures, an uncommon practice in medical education in North America at the time.

Reproduced by permission of the Osler Library of the History of Medicine, McGill University.

Practicing and Teaching

Osler returned to Ontario, Canada, in 1874, where he practiced medicine for a time before accepting an invitation to teach at McGill University. He quickly rose in rank from lecturer to Professor of the Institutes of Medicine, which encompassed histology, pathology, and physiology. Osler also lectured in pathology, physiology, and helminthology to veterinary students at the Montreal Veterinary College. He conducted postmortem demonstrations on all species of domestic animals as part of his early morning routine. He recognized the importance of comparative studies of people and animals and stressed that whatever branch of medicine (human or veterinary) a student followed, instruction in general medicine and comparative anatomy and pathology should be part of the curriculum. "Comparative medicine" were his bywords.

During his 10 years in Montreal, he taught both human and veterinary medical students, conducted more than 1,000 autopsies, and treated patients in the wards. His early interest in microscopy carried into his teaching career, and he offered special voluntary classes in microscopy at McGill.

Osler contributed to the veterinary literature with ten scientific papers and numerous editorial comments on animal diseases. He was the first to describe verminous bronchitis (*Filaroides osleri [Oslerus osleri]*), which bears his name. He investigated Pictou cattle disease, described the contagious nature of bovine tuberculosis, and advocated for instituting a meat inspection program (with particular emphasis on trichinosis and cysticercosis) in Montreal. He also described an outbreak of hog cholera (mistakenly called pig typhoid or anthrax by others) in Quebec in 1878. Osler's work on hog cholera is considered one of the earliest and best contributions to the understanding of the pathology of that disease.

Osler served as President of the Montreal Veterinary Medical Association from 1879 to 1880 and was one of the most active members, frequently presenting pathologic specimens from animals and people. On two occasions, he delivered the inaugural address at the Montreal Veterinary College, one on the relationship of animals to man and the other on comparative pathology. Together with Duncan MacEachran, an Edinburgh-trained veterinarian who established the Montreal Veterinary College, he promoted

Reproduced by permission of the Osler Library of the History of Medicine, McGill University.

the incorporation of the College into McGill University and suggested the designation "Faculty of Comparative Medicine and Veterinary Science." Osler defined pathology as "the physiology and microscopic anatomy of disease," which was truly an enlightened view during a time when many considered pathology simply "morbid anatomy."

Osler contributed to the concept of One Medicine, an idea originated by Virchow, who coined the term zoonoses. One Medicine is an integration and advancement of human and animal health by physicians and veterinarians working together. Today, the need for scientists who appreciate the connection between people and animals, particularly with the growing recognition of emerging diseases, zoonoses, and pandemics, is as vital as ever.

Expansion of Influence in the United States

In 1884, Osler was elected a fellow of the Royal College of Physicians and began a 5-year period as Professor of Clinical Medicine at the University of Pennsylvania, where he continued his intensive work in pathology while expanding his clinical activities. He also maintained his interest in veterinary medicine and joined the editorial board of the *Journal of Comparative Medicine and Veterinary Archives*. In 1889, Osler became the foundation Professor of Medicine, the first head of medicine at Johns Hopkins Hospital in Baltimore, where he taught alongside Drs. William Welch (pathology), William Steward Halsted (surgery), and Howard A. Kelly (gynecology). These preeminent physicians were captured in John Singer Sargent's famous and iconic 1905 painting "The Four Doctors."

It was at Johns Hopkins that Osler developed an international reputation as a brilliant physician and teacher with innovative approaches to medical education. He began the modern era of medicine as we know it today. He introduced bedside teaching to medicine, combining scientific knowledge and clinical skill, and developed a system of postgraduate training and education that is still used today. He introduced precise laboratory methods and exact science into the field of clinical medicine while retaining "humanism." He was a

Reproduced by permission of The Alan Mason Chesney Medical Archives of The Johns Hopkins Medical Institutions.

superb diagnostician, and he insisted on hospital patients being treated as human beings and not as "interesting cases."

In 1892 at the age of 43, Osler published the first edition of his renowned text, *The Principles and Practice of Medicine*, which had an enormous influence on medicine for more than 40 years. The book was notable for its "therapeutic conservatism." Osler criticized the futility of many of the then-available medicines—

comments that were generally true—and his demand for proof of efficacy before using a drug or medication is still relevant today. Although his other interests diverted him from publishing further in the veterinary field, he included many examples of comparative pathology in this text.

Career Transition from the United States to the United Kingdom

In 1905 at the age of 56, Osler left Baltimore suffering from overwork and exhaustion, accepting the invitation to become Regius Professor of Medicine at Oxford University in England. Although this was the highest medical position in Great Britain, it was supposed to be a relatively quiet situation clinically, allowing Osler a time to rest and write and to retire gradually. However, true to his dedication to his work and an inability to say "no," this turned out not to be the case. He named his home in Oxford "The Open Arms," where he frequently entertained students, physicians, and "friends of friends." During his 14 years in England, he exerted considerable influence on English medicine and on founding societies and journals, such as the Association of Physicians of Great Britain and Ireland and its *Quarterly Journal of Medicine*

Reproduced by permission of the Osler Library of the History of Medicine, McGill University.

(currently published as *An International Journal of Medicine*).
He worked hard to eradicate ill feeling in the medical profession,
fought against antivivisectionists, and promoted public health
measures of all kinds. In recognition of his work, he was knighted
a Baronet in 1911, thus becoming Sir William Osler.

In 1917, his son Edward was killed while serving with the Royal
Artillery in World War I, a tragedy from which Osler never recovered.
Osler continued to write clinical articles and historical essays during
the final years of his life, repeatedly revising his texts. His health
progressively deteriorated, and he died of bronchopneumonia and
empyema on December 29, 1919, at the age of 70.

A Lifetime of Extraordinary Accomplishment

There are many facets to Sir William Osler's life. As a writer, his
bibliography exceeds 1,500 items. He published many accounts
of his original scientific work in various journals, introducing a
style of writing that was clear and precise, yet literate and readable.
Osler was the first to describe platelet morphology. He also wrote
classical papers on hereditary telangiectasia (Osler-Weber-Rendu
disease), lupus erythematosus, and polycythemia vera (Osler-
Vaquez disease), always acknowledging the work of others. Osler
was interested in all types of cardiac disease, and his writings on
chronic infectious endocarditis contained descriptions of what are
still referred to as Osler's nodes. Of his nonscientific publications,
two of his essays, "A Way of Life" and "Aequinimatus," are still
considered meaningful and pertinent reading for medical students.

Osler's reputation as an astute clinician and talented preceptorial
teacher grew rapidly across the continent. His essential strength
was his ability to inspire and influence students and postgraduate
fellows. The magnitude of his influence on the medical profession
had not been seen before and has never been equaled since. Of his
many ideals, three recurring themes appear in his essays: doing
the day's work well and not bothering about tomorrow, always

Reproduced by permission of the Osler Library of the History of Medicine, McGill University.

being courteous and considerate to patients and professional colleagues, and cultivating a feeling of equanimity. In his evaluation of Osler's continued influence on medicine, the medical historian Roland concludes that it is related to the "contemporary resurgence of belief in the importance of humanism in restoring art to today's scientific physician."

Osler was an avid book collector and inspired his students to read widely in history and literature. His list of recommended books included one of his favorites, the *Religio Medici* by Sir Thomas Browne. He was keenly supportive of medical history and founded the Society for the Study of the History of Medicine. He bequeathed his historical and priceless library to McGill University, his alma mater. It took many years to catalog Osler's collection of approximately 8,000 titles, and the Osler Library (*"Bibliotheca Osleriana"*) did not officially open until May 1929.

Osler's Words and Influence Live On

Interest in Osler's life and writings was taken up by medical students at McGill University, who conceived the idea of forming a group as an inexpensive mechanism of pursuing and exchanging Osler's books and historical writings. The Osler Society of McGill University had its inaugural meeting on April 26, 1921. Numerous other associations have followed suit, including Osler House (Oxford University Clinical Medical Students Club), Osler Club of London, Osler Club of McMaster University (Canada), John P. McGovern Academy of Oslerian Medicine (University of Texas Medical Branch at Galveston), Osler Society of Greater Kansas

Student Society, Osler Society of New York, and the American Osler Society (AOS). Members of the AOS include medical professionals, medical historians, veterinarians, and others. All share the common goal of "keeping alive the memory of William Osler, and keeping its members vigilantly attentive to the lessons found in his life and teachings," and "a continual reminder of his high principles of life and humanism in practice and to teach others of Osler's continuing inspiration."

Although a century has passed since Osler made his first contributions to veterinary education at the Montreal Veterinary College, his influence in veterinary medicine remains evident. Veterinarians owe a great debt to William Osler. He made contributions to veterinary pathology beginning with his early lectures in Montreal and through his students, who took his teachings with them to Cornell University and later to other universities in North America. He introduced the importance of comparative pathology, promoted the concept of One Medicine, and made significant contributions to the standards and methods of veterinary education. His encouragement of the close connection between physicians and veterinarians improved human and animal health and the understanding of their mutual diseases.

Further Reading

- Abbott, ME. Sir William Osler Memorial Number. Appreciations and Reminiscences with a Classified Annotated Bibliography. *Bulletin IX of the International Association of Medical Museums and Journal of Technical Methods.* Murray Printing Co., Ltd; 1926.

- American Osler Society. http://www.americanosler.org/

- Bliss M. *William Osler—A Life in Medicine.* Oxford University Press; 1999.

- Cardiff RD, Ward JM, Barthold SW. "One Medicine—One Pathology": are veterinary and human pathology prepared? *Lab Invest.* 2008;88:18–26.

- Cushing H. *The Life of Sir William Osler.* Oxford University Press; 1925.

- Dukes TW. Veterinary history: early Canadian microscopists with associations to veterinary medicine. *Can Vet J.* 1993;34:241–245.

- Firkin BG, Whitworth JA. *Dictionary of Medical Eponyms.* The Parthenon Publishing Group; 1987.

- Golden RL, Roland CG. *Sir William Osler—An Annotated Bibliography with Illustrations.* Norman Publishing; 1988.

- Gyles C. One Medicine, One Health, One World. *Can Vet J.* 2016;57:345–346.

- Hogan DB. Did Osler suffer from "paranoia antitherapeuticum baltimorensis"? A comparative content analysis of *The Principles and Practice of Medicine and Harrison's Principles of Internal Medicine,* 11th ed. *CMAJ.* 1999;161(7):842–845.

- Kahn LH, Kaplan B, Steele JH. Confronting zoonoses through closer collaboration between medicine and veterinary medicine (as "one medicine"). *Vet Ital.* 2007;43(1):5–19.

- Mitchell CA. A note on the early history of veterinary science in Canada. *Can J Comp Med.* 1939;3:276–281.

- Murphy DA. Osler, now a veterinarian. *Can Med Assoc J.* 1960;83: 32–35.

- The Osler Society of McGill University. *W.W. Francis. Tributes from His Friends on the Occasion of the Thirty-fifth Anniversary of the Osler Society of McGill University.* The Osler Society; 1956.

- Ranta LE. The crossroads of veterinary medicine and human medicine. *Can J Comp Med.* 1945;9(12):321–325.

- Rodin AE. *Oslerian Pathology. An Assessment and Annotated Atlas of Museum Specimens.* Coronado Press; 1981.

- Roland CG (ed). *Sir William Osler 1849–1919. A Selection for Medical Students.* The Hannah Institute for the History of Medicine; 1982.

- Roland CG. The palpable Osler: a study in survival. *Persp Biol Med.* 1984;27:299–313.

- Saunders LZ. Some pioneers in comparative medicine. *Can Vet J.* 1973;14:27–35.

- Saunders LZ. From Osler to Olafson. The evolution of veterinary pathology in North America. *Can J Vet Res.* 1987;51:1–26.

- Saunders LZ. In ever widening circles: Osler's influence on veterinary medicine in Sweden. *Can Vet J.* 1993;34:431–435.
- Saunders LZ. *A Bibliographical History of Veterinary Pathology.* Allen Press, Inc.; 1996.
- Schwabe CW. *Cattle, Priests, and Progress in Medicine.* University of Minnesota Press; 1978.
- Sigerist HE. *The Great Doctors. A Biographical History of Medicine.* Books for Libraries Press; 1933.
- Singer DRJ. Osler Centenary Papers: Osler as a medical leader. *Postgrad Med J.* 2019;95:647–651.
- Teigen PM. William Osler and comparative medicine. *Can Vet J.* 1984;25:400–405.

THE WAY OF
VETERINARY MEDICINE

OUR MISSION

Donald L. Noah, DVM, MPH, DACVPM

"Scientists, it is said, are of two kinds: those who make it possible and those who make it happen."

–W.W. Armistead

As a new graduate veterinarian, you should take great pride in your success as a student and have enthusiasm for your future career opportunities. At this point, you may feel you have a good handle on the mission of veterinary medicine in general and your specific responsibilities as a practitioner, regardless of your interest or specialty. Over time, however, you may experience that some of the overarching concepts you were taught in school may fade into the background as your daily duties and responsibilities require more and more of your waking moments.

Over the course of many years and in various roles in veterinary medicine (eg, private practice, military service, academia), I have become much more aware of, and comfortable with, the One Health elements of our veterinary mission that either were not clear to me initially or became degraded over time. I hope that you will maintain "situational awareness" of the mission of veterinary medicine—especially as it relates to the One Health concept.

Our Mission as Veterinarians

Foundational documents exist to guide our veterinary endeavors. These include state statutes/rules/practice acts, the AVMA Principles of Veterinary Medical Ethics, the "Golden Rule," and, perhaps most importantly, the Veterinarian's Oath. During my career as a veterinary academician, I have also had the opportunity to teach in several colleges of human medicine. I have found that in the academic world of human medicine, there is not a single Hippocratic-type oath that is used by all the medical schools in the United States. In fact, I found more than 30 different versions! In contrast, all the colleges of veterinary medicine in the United States adhere to the same Veterinarian's Oath, with all new members of our profession taking the Oath on graduation.

The Veterinarian's Oath

Being admitted to the profession of veterinary medicine, I solemnly swear to use my scientific knowledge and skills for the benefit of society through the protection of animal health and welfare, the prevention and relief of animal suffering, the conservation of animal resources, the promotion of public health, and the advancement of medical knowledge.

I will practice my profession conscientiously, with dignity, and in keeping with the principles of veterinary medical ethics.

I accept as a lifelong obligation the continual improvement of my professional knowledge and competence.

Notice not only the wording of our Oath, but also the order in which the words appear. For instance, the Oath directs us to apply our knowledge and skills first for the "benefit of society," not specifically for the health of the animal kingdom. I do not believe this word ordering was accidental at all. Although it originated before the recognition and expansion of the One Health concept, this Oath should remind us that the mission of veterinary medicine is to enhance all aspects of human society.

Brief Background of One Health

The origin of organized veterinary medicine may be rooted in the initiation of the first veterinary college in Lyon, France, in 1761. It didn't take long before the similarities between animal and human pathology were recognized. One of the more salient of those points of recognition occurred in 1856 when the German physician Rudolf Virchow famously stated, "Between animal and human medicine, there is no dividing line—nor should there be." While I doubt he meant that veterinarians and physicians were (or are) interchangeable, he certainly recognized the inherent similarities in mammalian pathology and medicine.

The next important milestone was the contribution of Sir William Osler, who taught in both medical and veterinary colleges in Canada in the late 1800s. It may surprise many of you to know that, in addition to being a significant contributor to human medicine, he established a novel (to say the least!) educational concept at McGill University in which students could complete a combined MD/DVM degree program in 5 years. This might come as less of a surprise when you realize that one of Dr. Osler's original mentors was Rudolf Virchow. Unfortunately, this dual-degree program was short-lived because Osler departed McGill University to become one of the four founding physicians of Johns Hopkins Hospital in Baltimore, Maryland.

The next major One Health milestone was the work of Dr. James Steele, who created the first veterinary public health division in 1947 in the Communicable Diseases Center (now the Centers for Disease Control and Prevention) in Atlanta, Georgia. His leadership resulted in national vaccination programs against such diseases as rabies and bovine brucellosis to name just a few. Widely regarded as the "father of veterinary public health," Dr. Steele's contributions are memorialized by the annual awarding of the American Veterinary Epidemiology Society's K.F. Meyer/James H. Steele Gold-Headed Cane Award.

Through this continuum of recognizing the similarity between human and animal pathology, this concept lacked an official moniker until the 1960s when Dr. Calvin Schwabe, founding chair of the Department of Epidemiology and Preventive Medicine at the UC Davis College of Veterinary Medicine, coined the term "One Medicine." This further highlighted the need for collaboration between human and animal health care providers, culminating in the most recent nomenclature—that of One Health, which incorporates the importance of considering the health of the environment alongside that of people and animals. The One Health concept was spearheaded by Dr. Roger Mahr, who, as president of the American Veterinary Medical Association, established the AVMA One Health Initiative Task Force in 2006. He later collaborated with the American Medical Association, resulting in their 2007 One Health resolution to promote partnering between veterinary and human medical organizations.

Relevancy of One Health to Practitioners

In my experience of leading and teaching the One Health concept in several American universities, I have often been asked by both faculty members and students (human medical and veterinary) this question: *"Okay, I understand the comprehensive scope of One Health…but what does it mean to me as a practitioner?"* My answer, regardless of the origin of the question, is this: When you see a patient, whether that patient is a single individual or a population, cast your mind beyond what is being learned and discussed in that exam room and guide your medical actions based on the following questions:

> *Where did the etiologic agent come from that is affecting this patient?*
>
> Not all pathogens are infectious, and not all etiologies will be apparent to you as a clinician. Regardless, you have a

responsibility to apply critical thinking and determine the most likely agent, behavior, or environmental condition that resulted in this particular problem.

How is my patient being affected by this agent and, in addition to the patient in front of me, who else (regardless of species) may be affected by this problem?

Too many of us focus solely on the patient in the room and fail to consider others that may be affected, be they on four legs or two. Remember that noncommunicable conditions, such as obesity, can also be affected or influenced by others in our patient's environment. You may have even observed an association between the degree of obesity between your animal patients and their client owners. As part of your therapeutic intervention, you might include the recommendation to take the pet for daily walks to increase metabolism and aerobic capacity. In doing so, are you treating not only your patient, but also perhaps contributing to the health and well-being of the owner?

Are there others who can assist in providing comprehensive care to this patient?

Please do not fall into the all-too-common trap of believing that you possess all the diagnostic and therapeutic expertise to deal with your patient's problem(s). Consider how the owner can assist in making the therapies you recommend more effective and longer lasting. Additionally, consider whether other health professionals can assist. These might include the owner's family physician or pediatrician in the case of a zoonotic disease or even a mental health provider to help your patient's human family deal with a debilitating illness or end-of-life condition in their pet.

Are there others (perhaps not even human) who can assist in helping this patient recover?

We are increasingly seeing the benefits of all sorts of animal-facilitated assistance and therapy. Leveraging the inherent value of the human-animal bond, these benefits also include emotional support. There is a long history of guide dogs assisting those with vision or hearing impairment, and dogs and other therapy animals assist people with chronic, debilitating, and end-of-life conditions. Finally, remember that even your animal patient may benefit from having another animal with which to bond and heal.

Further Reading

- Dunlop RH, Williams DJ. *Veterinary Medicine: An Illustrated History.* Mosby; 1996.
- Natterson B, Bowers K. *Zoobiquity.* Random House; 2013.

SCIENCE AND ART IN VETERINARY MEDICINE

Trevor R. Ames, DVM, MS, DACVIM

*"The practice of medicine is an art, not a trade; a calling,
not a business; a calling in which your heart will be exercised
equally with your head. The practice of medicine is an art,
based on science."*

–Sir William Osler

From the beginning of recorded history, there is evidence of man's attempts to understand, treat, and prevent disease. Ancient healers observed the causes, symptoms, and outcomes of the afflictions that plagued members of their communities and conducted experiments to attempt to cure maladies and heal injuries. Eventually, as observations were recorded and considered, conclusions were drawn as to the causes of disease, and the methods of managing disease became formalized. Similarly, early records of animal diseases were recorded with sufficient accuracy to document the methods of diagnosis, highlighting how certain individual observations led to the diagnosis of a specific ailment.

Ancient medicine evolved in unique ways in different parts of the world and was influenced by regional cultures and civilizations. Consider the evolution of eastern and western medicine, in which various methods of diagnosis and treatment were developed and practiced in both human and veterinary medical fields. The evolution of scientific discoveries and advances in biology, physics, and chemistry have influenced not only our understanding of the world in which we live, but also our tremendous progress in the field of medicine.

The Art of Medicine

Diagnosing disease and choosing the best therapy demands both scientific competency and technical skills. However, even with today's sophisticated diagnostic technology, the number of pharmaceutical and surgical options that will be successful in a given medical case is finite. In other words, scientific knowledge and technical ability alone are not sufficient for delivering optimal care. Success also requires that veterinarians (and all health care providers) exhibit the best traits of humanity, show empathy, and communicate well—the "art" of medicine. The ability to provide concern, sympathy, compassion, and to act as a resource of humane options are of considerable importance in the practice of veterinary medicine.

When clients become unhappy with the care that their animals have received, the problem can often be traced back to poor communication between the veterinarian and the client. For example, the veterinarian may not have informed the client of the limitations of available treatments or provided that information at the appropriate time (before treatment is undertaken). Successful communication is vital to a positive health care outcome for a patient or a herd or flock. Often, veterinarians fail to listen, or perhaps understand, their clients and begin a course of therapy that is either less than the client expected or more than they can afford. In another scenario, veterinarians may practice the highest quality of medicine and have the desired results, yet poor communication skills may give the client the impression that the veterinarian did not care about their animals or did not listen to their concerns. The animal may be healthy, but the client remains dissatisfied with the entire relationship. Students will learn that the topics they currently regard as difficult, such as memorizing the autonomic nervous system, will become second nature with experience. In contrast, the "soft skills," such as client communication and maintaining interpersonal relationships, are more challenging.

Sound judgment also falls under the umbrella of the art of medicine. Sound judgment leads the clinician to consider the obvious first, rather than the rare exceptions. The wisdom of the English friar and philosopher William of Ockham (c. 1285/7–1347) is evident in "Occam's Razor," his theory that the simplest solution is most likely the right one. Theodore Woodward (1914–2005), a noted researcher and educator at the University of Maryland School of Medicine, is credited with saying, "If you hear hoof beats, think of horses not zebras," an adage that is warmly regarded by veterinarians. Sound judgment also implies that we be systematic, thorough, and diligent in performing patient examinations because it is easier to overlook signs when we are inconsistent. In addition, differentials may not be considered if assumptions are made. In the words of Thomas McCrae, a student of Osler's, "You miss more for not looking than you do for not knowing."

In many professions, success is enhanced by how we present ourselves, which is vital in our interactions with both clients and colleagues. Our demeanor and how we dress, speak, and act, influences how our audience perceives our message. The art of presentation is a needed skill for within practice settings, academic institutions, government agencies, and corporations. Those who excel in presentation may be seen as naturally blessed, but preparation and practice can enable any presenter to be effective and well received.

The Science of Medicine
It is easy to see an association between medicine and science. Advanced diagnostic imaging, laboratory techniques, analysis of

therapeutic outcomes, and population data to optimize treatments all come to mind. These advances are all rooted in science, which continually evolves. Any experienced clinician can remember pathophysiologic mechanisms, clinical examination techniques, and treatment protocols that were widely accepted as the standard of care in days past but have now been disproved or fallen by the wayside as the understanding of diseases and therapies improve. B.M. Hegde, a cardiologist and former Vice Chancellor of Manipal University, stated it well in that scientific truths are not true for all times and that today's truth may become tomorrow's folly. The half-life of truth in medicine is short and getting shorter. Dr. Charles Burwell, a cardiologist and past dean of Harvard Medical School, said, "Half of what we are going to teach you is wrong, and half of it is right. Our problem is that we don't know which half is which." Respecting the science of veterinary medicine requires lifelong learning to stay abreast of the latest advances.

The Debate

Clinicians who believe that art trumps science in medicine will point out that every patient and every client are different, and so there is no single way to manage a case. They believe that compliance with treatment algorithms is "cookbook medicine" and that clinicians should be able to chart their own course when treating a patient.

Other clinicians who view medical care as an applied science oppose this viewpoint. These clinicians argue that today's sophisticated information technologies, advanced diagnostic tools, and scientific advances can be used to create guidelines that result in improved clinical outcomes. They also assert that variation in the care given to various patients reflects obsolete thinking and leads to poorer patient outcomes.

Evidence-based treatment protocols have been developed in human medicine for managing patients with myriad conditions, eg, acute stroke, myocardial infarction, etc. Although veterinary medicine lags behind human medicine in development of these protocols, the body of veterinary knowledge is growing rapidly. Veterinary practitioners who ignore the scientific evidence and favor their own intuition do so at the risk of the quality of care they provide to their patients and clients, their livelihoods, their reputations and possibly the reputation of the veterinary profession as a whole. Adhering to the latest scientific veterinary guidelines also enables us to be good stewards of vital resources (such as antimicrobial drugs) and to ensure that food of animal origin is safe and wholesome.

Remaining Challenges

The most successful practitioners know how to use their artistic skills to communicate and advocate with and for their patients while using the wealth of available information to guide them in the practice of veterinary medicine. However, there is a growing concern in veterinary medicine that students are being taught only how to deliver the most complex, highest standard of care rather than how to offer a continuum or spectrum of care. An obese dog with disk disease may still benefit from weight loss, controlled exercise, and NSAID therapy if the client cannot afford surgery. Similarly, a cat with ill-defined symptoms may benefit from symptomatic care if extensive diagnostic testing is beyond what the client can support. Overreliance on expensive testing and recommending only costly therapeutic options may limit care for many animal patients and/or create economic hardship for the animal's owner.

In both veterinary and human medicine, there may be barriers to optimal care that limit the ability to achieve a successful outcome. In some cases, the same obstacles that influence public health outcomes also impact the health and well-being of animals and pet owners. Veterinary training acknowledges the interconnectedness of people, animals, and the environment, but the concept of social determinants of health is much newer in veterinary medicine. Thus, few veterinarians feel adept at supporting the well-being of the entire household. Conversely, nursing and social work practitioners are highly skilled in these areas. However, they may be unaware that animals can impact clients' abilities to access health and social services or that animals can serve as untapped motivators for clients to make healthy changes in their own lives. A new opportunity for veterinary medicine may include networking and communicating with other health care professionals to address important health disparities among resource-limited pet owners by using a multidisciplinary team approach that values the importance of the human-animal bond, equitable care, and accessible services.

Skillful collaboration and networking opportunities will also exist for other sectors of veterinary medicine. As the public becomes more aware of how and where their food is produced, food animal practitioners will need to collaborate with environmental scientists and behaviorists to provide animal protein sustainably and humanely. Wildlife veterinarians will have success only if they work closely with ecosystem specialists to understand the effects of human encroachment, invasive species, and climate change on wildlife health and habitat. Participating as a successful team member will require understanding the roles and responsibilities within the team as well as how to communicate between team members. Interprofessional practice will become a new way in which art and science interact for veterinary medicine.

Further Reading

• Achterberg J. What is medicine? *Altern Ther Health Med.* 1996;2(3):58–61.

• Haynes AB, et al. A surgical safety checklist to reduce morbidity and mortality in a global population. *N Engl J Med.* 2009;360:491–499.

- Hegde BM. Science and the art of medicine. *J Indian Acad Clin Med.* 1999;4:1–3. www.indegen.com/main/issues/indIsses11.asp

- Lakshmipati G. *Care of the Medical Outpatient.* (Preface) 1st ed. 2003. Nama publication, Coimbatore, Tamil Nadu, India.

- Panda SC. Medicine: science or art? *Mens Sana Monogr.* 2006;4(1):127–138.

- Saunders J. The practice of clinical medicine as an art and a science. *Med Humanit.* 2000;26(1):18–22.

- Schaffer J. What to not multiply without necessity. *Austral J Philo.* 2015;93:4:644–664.

ANIMAL WELFARE

Abbie Viscardi, PhD

"We can judge the heart of a man by his treatment of animals."

–Immanuel Kant

Recognition of animal welfare as a scientific field of study began in 1964, when Ruth Harrison wrote *Animal Machines,* a book describing intensive livestock production systems that became common after World War II. At the time, the public was largely unaware of the shift in animal production from family farming to industrial farming, and the result was public outrage regarding the unethical treatment of farm animals. In response, the British government appointed a committee of agriculturalists and scientists to investigate the welfare of animals kept in intensive livestock production systems.

Developing Frameworks

In 1965, the Brambell Report was drafted and provided specific recommendations for animal husbandry. It called for research in animal science and behavior, stress physiology, and veterinary medicine to improve our understanding of how different production systems influenced an animal's welfare. Most importantly, this report outlined five fundamental freedoms that all animals should enjoy:

- Freedom from hunger and thirst
- Freedom from discomfort
- Freedom from pain, injury, or disease

- Freedom to express normal behavior
- Freedom from fear and distress

These five freedoms became the first framework used to assess animal welfare, and it is still used today in animal welfare audits and in writing animal care protocols. It is also used in veterinary clinical practice to develop appropriate treatment plans and to make end-of-life decisions.

Over 30 years later in 1997, Drs. David Fraser, Dan Weary, Ed Pajor, and Barry Milligan introduced another animal welfare framework: the Three Circles Model, which consists of the following concepts:

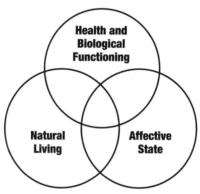

Basic health and functioning: Animals should have normal body functioning, growth, and development, and be in good health.

Affective state: This refers to the emotional state of the animal; positive emotions, such as pleasure and contentment, should be promoted, while negative emotions, including fear, hunger and pain, should be minimized.

Natural living: Animals should be able to perform natural behaviors and have access to natural elements, including fresh air and sunshine.

These concepts are not mutually exclusive and can overlap. Animals can be in situations or systems that satisfy some, but not all, of the core elements of this model.

Additional Welfare Considerations

Historically, veterinarians have prioritized the health and biological functioning of the animals in their care, while placing less emphasis on the animal's emotions (ie, how the animal feels) or on supporting the animal's ability to perform natural behaviors. While animal health is essential to veterinary medicine, an animal's overall welfare encompasses other critical considerations.

Consider an active dog who is crated for 90% of the day or a young cat who is chased and terrorized daily by children in the household. Both these animals have access to fresh water and food and are biologically healthy. If we only considered the health of the animal, we would conclude that both the dog and the cat are doing well and possibly thriving. However, most of us would not come to this conclusion when other aspects of the animal's home environment are considered. A multifaceted, holistic approach is needed to accurately assess animal welfare.

Challenges in Assessments and Decisions

Integrating animal welfare assessments into veterinary medicine is challenging because these decision-making tools are not black or white, right or wrong. Many of the cases you encounter will be in the gray area. Your colleagues may look at the same situation and come to very different conclusions about the animal's welfare. Divergent opinions are often rooted in differences in ethical beliefs regarding animal care. For example, an individual aligned with a utilitarian perspective will have views that differ significantly from an individual with an animal rights sensibility. In many cases, neither perspective will be wrong. So, what do we do when faced with an ethical dilemma in animal welfare? Unfortunately, there is no easy answer. There may be times when you must challenge yourself to set aside your personal beliefs and determine what is best from the animal's point of view.

In large animal medicine, animal welfare assessments are complicated by the fact that different standards of care exist for animals housed in different environments or locations. For example, a large layer poultry operation will have different animal welfare requirements and audits to meet the standards of some egg purchasers than will layer poultry raised on a small farm or in an urban backyard. Best practices for these layers are different from best practices for broilers, turkeys, swine, dairy cattle, beef cattle, etc. When called on to make animal welfare assessments, veterinarians should be knowledgeable about the species-specific care requirements to ensure they are providing an accurate report. In some serious cases, you may need to provide your professional opinion regarding an animal welfare case in a court of law. If you feel uncomfortable in making a contested assessment, you may want to defer or refer to a veterinarian experienced in this area.

In small animal medicine, consider a senior dog that has been diagnosed with a treatable cancer. The dog's health has been declining in recent years, before the cancer diagnosis. Because the cancer is treatable, the veterinarian and owner may be inclined to pursue treatment options. But is putting a senior dog through surgery, chemotherapy, and/or radiation in the dog's best interest? Could this lead to undue suffering? What will the dog's quality of life be during and after treatment? Will animal welfare be reduced? Prolonging an animal's life does not necessarily mean that the animal's quality of life is good. In this case, euthanasia may be the most humane option. Just because we can treat an animal's illness does not mean we *should*. Remember, "protection of animal health and welfare and the prevention and relief of animal suffering" are key components in the Veterinarian's Oath and should be considered in every problematic case you encounter.

The Million Dollar Question

At the core of many animal welfare discussions is this question: *What constitutes a good life for animals?* Because animals cannot tell us what they need to live a good life, we must rely on advancements in animal welfare to develop our understanding of this critical topic. As is true of any scientific field, there is always more to discover and learn in the quest to improve animal welfare. Veterinarians must be committed to lifelong learning and be open to integrating newly acquired information and techniques into veterinary practice.

Another common question in the field of animal welfare is this: *Does this animal have a life worth living?* This question is central to welfare discussions of farm, zoo, and laboratory animals, and it can also be applied to companion animals. If you determine an animal is in poor health or chronically stressed and does not *currently* have a life worth living, what can you do to improve it? Would treating an underlying illness or disease lead to a better life for the animal? What short- and long-term impacts are expected after treatment (eg, pain, mobility, separation, stress) that could reduce the animal's quality of life?

The magnitude of these changes will differ based on the individual animal. Although animal welfare is discussed in general terms across species and breeds, the individual animal (eg, personality, behavior) must always be considered when making assessments and drawing conclusions. For example, my black lab becomes depressed when she cannot go for her daily walks; therefore, restricting her ability to exercise would have a much greater impact on her quality of life than that of a less active dog.

What Is Your Responsibility?

If an animal is consistently seen in a state of poor welfare, it is your job to educate the owner about proper animal care, handling, and treatment. However, if you have reason to suspect that the animal is being mistreated (abused or neglected) and the owner is not complying with your requests to improve the animal's quality of life, you may be legally mandated to report this to the appropriate authority. Laws differ by state. You should familiarize yourself with your state's legislative standards on reporting, confidentiality of veterinary records, and liability considerations as soon as possible, so you are prepared to act if you encounter a case of abuse or neglect. The American Veterinary Medical Association (AVMA) has some excellent resources to guide you through this process. Your state veterinary medical association can also be an excellent resource for guidance and direction in legal considerations. While reporting may be uncomfortable for you, especially if you have a good relationship with the owner, remember that you are obliged to protect the animals in your care; if you do not speak up, the animal may continue to suffer or meet an untimely demise. By reporting, you are giving the animal a chance to experience good health and quality of life, minimal stress, and contentment—in other words, having a life worth living.

According to the AVMA, *"Ensuring animal welfare is a human responsibility that includes consideration for all aspects of animal well-being, including proper housing, management, nutrition, disease prevention and treatment, responsible care, humane handling, and, when necessary, humane euthanasia."* We have seen a shift in veterinarians taking a more balanced approach to animal care, considering more than just good animal health and biological functioning. Veterinarians want to provide the highest standard of care for their patients. Improving animal welfare both inside and outside the clinic will go a long way toward achieving that goal.

Further Reading

- American Veterinary Medical Association. Abuse reporting requirements by state. Accessed Jan 10, 2021. https://www.avma.org/resources-tools/animal-health-welfare/abuse-reporting-requirements-state

- Brambell R. Report of the Technical Committee to enquire into the welfare of animals kept under intensive livestock husbandry systems (Brambell Report). Command Paper 2836, Her Majesty's Stationery Office, London, England; 1965.

- Fraser D. *Understanding Animal Welfare: The Science in its Cultural Context.* John Wiley & Sons Ltd.; 2008.

- Fraser D, Weary DM, Pajor EA, et al. A scientific conception of animal welfare that reflects ethical concerns. *Anim Welfare.* 1997;6:187–205.

PROFESSIONALISM AND PROFESSIONAL IDENTITY

Lonnie J. King, DVM, MS, MPA, DACVPM

"Life isn't about finding yourself. Life is about creating yourself."

–George Bernard Shaw

Students begin their veterinary medical education with an incomplete understanding of the many roles that veterinarians perform, the skills needed to excel and serve, and the ethical dilemmas they are sure to face over their careers. While we all understand the need for acquiring medical and scientific knowledge and developing clinical competency, these are, by themselves, insufficient to ensure your future success and personal fulfillment. How you apply your knowledge is equally critical. Your integrity, ethical conduct, and values will define who you are and create the moral compass that is necessary to prepare you for your life's work and the profound responsibilities of a doctor of veterinary medicine. With this recognition, your education and training must involve both your mind and your heart.

To better appreciate this dichotomy, you should consider several terms that are commonly used in veterinary medicine but are often poorly understood. First, you are joining a profession, which is defined as a calling requiring specialized knowledge and intensive training. Second, you are becoming a professional, meaning that you are expected to conform to appropriate standards and to adhere to certain codes of conduct and ethical principles. Third, society and the veterinary medical profession have established expectations for your behavior and actions that underpin the trust and confidence that others have conferred on you. These beliefs and your conduct are termed professionalism. Veterinary medicine has earned and enjoyed the trust and confidence of the public based on the professionalism exhibited by its members. It is a status that is hard to earn but easily lost, and it should never be taken for granted. Last, you must develop a professional identity. Your professional identity defines who you are and incorporates compassion, reflection, self-awareness, core values, and ethical standards. Professional identity grounds you, guides you, and becomes a reliable, steady hand to help direct your decision-making and ability to address moral dilemmas and competing interests.

Professional identity and professionalism are not synonymous. Your professional identity is the manifestation of professionalism and is formed at the individual level. In contrast, professionalism is constructed by the communities you serve and your peers within the veterinary medical society. The figure illustrates the relationships among these entities and the broad scope of societal responsibilities and obligations recognized and accepted in the life of a veterinarian. Note that your professional identity is the centerpiece of all these connections; it defines you personally and professionally and will determine your success and legacy.

Forming a Professional Identity

The formation of your professional identity begins on the first day of your veterinary medical education as a student. It develops over time and culminates at a point when your values and norms are internalized, ultimately resulting in how you think, act, and feel like a distinguished doctor of veterinary medicine. The formation of your professional identity is a transformative journey in which you integrate the knowledge, skills, behaviors, and values of a

Public Health   Food Safety and Security   Animal Welfare

PROFESSIONALISM
Expected behavior
Conduct
Attitude

PROFESSION
Your calling

Continuous
Learning

Species
Conservation

**PROFESSIONAL
IDENTITY**
Who you uniquely are
Internalization of values
Norms
Sense of self
Individual manifestation of
professionalism

Knowledge
and Skills

Prevent
Suffering

Advancing
Knowledge

Animal
Health/Care

VETERINARIAN'S OATH
Promise to society
Aspiration

PROFESSIONAL
Conforming to standards
Adhering to codes

One Health   Wildlife   Ecosystem Sustainability competent and humanistic veterinarian and create your unique character. Acquiring a professional identity is a continual process that evolves through mentorship, emulation of role models, self-reflection, and the build-up of experiences over time that affirm the best practices of our traditions and ethics. After your 4 years in veterinary college, you will graduate with a new value system, a sense of self, and a fully developed moral compass that will be very different from when you started.

There is a growing concern that veterinary students and veterinarians may, at times, be disproportionately affected by poor emotional health and well-being. Veterinary medicine is an intensely caring profession; its members are powerfully compassionate, empathetic, and kind. Yet, concurrently, our careers are rooted in complex, rapidly changing times and challenging social circumstances. Thus, your professional identity must also include self-awareness, self-care, and reflection. It is imperative that you practice self-care by learning and embracing coping skills and resiliency. If you do not, you will be unable to deliver the excellent care and services that your patients, clients, and organizations expect and deserve. Your professional identity is central to defining who you are and must include your personal health and well-being. We cannot genuinely care about our patients, our work, and each other without first caring about ourselves. Being good at caring about both others and yourself is not mutually exclusive and is an essential component of your professional identity.

Professions Shaped by History

Both human and veterinary medicine have been shaped by history, mythology, symbolism, and oaths. The Code of Hammurabi was a set of laws created by the Babylonians in the 18th century BC and was the first code to deal with all aspects of society, including medicine. The Hippocratic Oath, one of history's oldest binding documents, was written by Hippocrates almost 2500 years ago and is still sworn to by physicians today as they strive to set their medical standards and continue strong traditions.

Like human medicine, veterinary medicine has adopted meaningful symbols from Greek mythology. The veterinary logo depicts Asclepius's rod; he was the Greek god of healing and medicine, and his staff or rod represents the healing arts and is shown with a single serpent coiled around it. Because the serpent sheds its skin, it symbolizes both renewal and rejuvenation and, because it is poisonous, it also symbolizes the duality of your work dealing with life and death. The letter "V" is superimposed over the figure to signify the profession of veterinary medicine. According to mythology, Asclepius was the son of the god Apollo and pupil of the centaur Chiron, who was famous for his wisdom and knowledge of medicine. While the logo and symbols have professional  significance, they do not come with magical powers of immediate transformation. You will definitely be transformed through time, education and experience, and you will learn to appreciate the ancient legends and meaningful vows embedded in our history. This is part of our extraordinary legacy that is imbued with honor and acknowledges the responsibilities necessary to becoming an esteemed member of the veterinary profession.

The Veterinarian's Oath (see Our Mission, p XX) was officially adopted by the American Veterinary Medical Association in 1954 and has undergone several changes since then. Our oath is unique because of its broad scope of obligations and because it represents the most altruistic of all the health professions. It is our social contract and public promise to those we serve, and we further vow that we will use our knowledge and skills to accomplish these public services. The Veterinarian's Oath and the veterinary logo are foundations that venerate and honor the past but also serve as a strong beacon directing your future.

A Way of Life

Choosing a veterinary career is also choosing a way of life. The life of a veterinary student has similarities to your future professional life. You will encounter challenges, difficulties, humility, exhilaration, frustration, and the normal ups and downs experienced by everyone. However, you will find a life of meaning, service, and purpose shared by only a very few. In summary, knowing that you are, or will soon be a doctor of veterinary medicine, you should understand how the following factors will define you and how you will serve and care for others throughout your entire career.

- You are a member of the veterinary profession, which is a special calling that we all share.
- You will be expected to conform to certain standards and codes that will define you as a professional.
- You will gain an understanding of the concept of professionalism that will guide your behavior and actions.
- You will swear to the Veterinarian's Oath, which will direct and inspire your life's work and establish a social contract.
- You will comprehend the importance of our historical background, symbolism, and meaning.
- You will thoughtfully develop a professional identity to sustain and ground you as you internalize the essential norms and values enabling you to think, act, and feel like a doctor of veterinary medicine.

Further Reading

- Cruess RL, Cruess SR, Boudreau JD, et al. Reframing medical education to support professional identity formation. *Acad Med.* 2014;89(11):1446–14451.

- Hodgson JL, Pelzer JM. *Veterinary Medical Education: A Practical Guide.* Wiley-Blackwell, 2017.

- MacKenzie CR. Professionalism and medicine. *HSS J.* 2007;3(2):222–227.

- National Association of Colleges and Employers: Career Readiness Competencies, Result of Employer Survey, 2014. Available at https://www.naceweb.org/career-readiness/competencies/career-readiness-competencies-employer-survey-results/

GENERATIONAL CHANGE

Eleanor M. Green, DVM, DACVIM, DABVP

*"Each generation imagines itself to be more intelligent than
the one that went before it, and wiser than the one
that comes after it."*

–George Orwell

Ready or not, Generation Z is entering the workforce and the veterinary profession. Gen Z enters on the heels of the millennials, who challenged the status quo, just like every generation before them.

For the first time in history, there are five generations in the workplace: Generation Z, the millennials, Generation X, the baby boomers, and the last of the Silent Generation. Differences in age and generation create a diversity of thought and perspective, which poses a few challenges but creates even more opportunities. Diverse workplaces consistently outperform their competitors. People who feel heard, understood, and valued are more likely to fully invest themselves in a workplace. The key to success is understanding and leveraging differences, including generational differences, to optimize personal achievements, thriving businesses, and the future for us all.

As Stephen Covey says, *"Seek first to understand and then to be understood."* Many resources are available to further the appreciation of generational differences, their values, beliefs, and opinions, which can promote mutual understanding. The responsibility for doing so lies within all the generations. Recently, some have challenged the theories of generations, believing that generational differences are a myth and that there are more similarities than differences. While caution is necessary to avoid stereotyping, which can result in false assumptions about individuals, varying experiences and societal circumstances influence different individuals and generations, so the variances are worth exploring. Recognizing generational trends may improve communications, tolerance, and understanding.

Millennials (1980–2000)

Millennials currently outnumber other generations and, as a group, exhibit some common attributes. They will go through all the life stages of previous generations but are predicted to do so at an older age; for example, they will marry and have children later in life. Many consider their pets as starter families, and some choose pets over children as their permanent families. Millennials own more pets than other generations, which will give them substantial influence on the pet industry and pet health care. This influence is growing by leaps and bounds because of their numbers and spending power.

Millennials approach work-life balance differently than baby boomers. Their work ethic is strong but manifests as being highly functional when at work and playing hard when not at work. They are "connectors" and crave feedback. They have a strong devotion to causes, and their social consciousness is sharp, both as veterinarians and as clients.

Millennials comprise the first generation to enjoy unprecedented access in the most high-tech, innovative environment in history. They can search the world's information, launch a business remotely, create a freelance business, leverage crowdsourced funding, create community test ideas, and much more. Access has changed how millennials learn, communicate, network, socialize, and build businesses. They are entrepreneurial.

Millennials are considered the first global generation and have more in common with their international peers than any previous generation. As such, their effect on the globalization of veterinary medicine may be profound. The disruption caused by the millennials, and that predicted for Gen Z, is substantial and will be enhanced by our exponentially changing world.

Generation Z (2000–present)

Gen Z will have a profound effect on the veterinary profession, especially in terms of innovation, business models, and technologies. Gen Z is also known as the iGeneration or Digital Natives. More than any other generation to date, they have no problem using the latest technologies and platforms. They have grown up in an on-demand culture with ubiquitous connectivity and limitless interests and avenues for learning. Rapid advancements in technology, mobile devices, social networks, and overall connectivity have exposed them to more life-shaping content than any previous generation. They use countless platforms to connect, consume, and contribute. This boundary-less generation communicates and collaborates globally, from real-time gaming to actual work with peers around the world. Gen Z contributes to the exponential power of new trends, products, and services to reach and reshape generations. They exploit their traits as self-starters, self-learners, and self-motivators to make their mark on the world. Part of their legacy will be influencing the behavior of previous generations who strive to remain relevant in a high-technology world. While humanity has always looked to its youth for innovation, in our current exponentially changing world, Gen Z will substantially influence how we all live and work. As technology and connectivity rapidly evolve, so will emerging generations.

Response to Change

Gen Z's adaptability underscores the powerful difference among generations in response to change. Gen Z has grown up in a rapidly changing world where even the rate of change is increasing, so change is a way of life. Gen X often perceives change as vehicles for new opportunities and thus, may embrace change more readily. Baby boomers tend to prefer a stable work environment, so it seems they are also more likely to resist change. The hardworking silent generation, also known as the traditionalists, value conformity. All generations must acknowledge the growing importance of adaptability in today's exponentially changing world; in fact, some predict that one's "adaptability quotient" is rapidly becoming more important for success than the intelligence quotient or even emotional intelligence.

The Multigenerational Workforce

Heads up, Generation Z and millennials! Currently, the baby boomers dominate leadership roles, control 70% of the disposable income in the United States, and are choosing to stay in the workforce longer, retiring later in life. They are twice as likely as millennials to launch a new business.

Those in leadership roles face particular challenges and opportunities to relate to and deal with five diverse generations in the workplace. We all must interact effectively with bosses and coworkers and maneuver within the workplace culture, which typically starts at the top. The chart below summarizes generational differences and can serve as a quick reference to understand motivations and preferences. In the end, an essential key to preventing both generation and personal tension is understanding and valuing differences, as well as similarities.

Remember that veterinary medicine is about not only healing animals but also interacting effectively with people. The principles of generational differences are relevant for dealing with colleagues, staff members, and, of course, clients. Creating the optimal client experience hinges on understanding clients' individual needs and desires. Although Generation Alpha (2010–present) is very young, many children accompany their parents during their pet's appointment, and clients often appreciate the veterinarian speaking to the child as well. Effectively doing so will not only generate good will but also create a robust and diverse population of young people seeking careers in veterinary medicine.

What will the veterinary profession, including its culture, look like in the future? Veterinary medicine should mirror the diverse population in which it exists, including all definitions of diversity. The profession will be shaped predominantly by the people within it, as they effectively adapt and thrive within an exponentially changing world. As innovations in human healthcare and healthy lifestyles allow people to live and work longer than ever before, the richness of generations sharing the workplace will become even more prevalent and have more impact. All generations will pool their knowledge, experiences, and perspectives to contribute to tackling the challenges of the world, the veterinary profession, and life. But for tomorrow, our profession is in the hands of the newer generations, and they can most certainly be trusted to make it better.

> *"The young do not know enough to be prudent, and therefore they attempt the impossible—and achieve it, generation after generation."*
>
> –Pearl S. Buck

Generational Differences

	Silent Generation	Boomers	Gen X	Millennial	Gen Z
Birth dates (approximate)	1900-1946	1946-1965	1965-1979	1980-2000	2000-present
Synonyms/ description	Greatest generation, G.I. generation, veterans, the forgotten generation	Me generation, beat generation, moral authority	Latchkey generation, MTV generation, the doers	Gen Y, first digitals, echo boomers	iGen, centennials
Attributes	Experience, dedication, loyalty, emotional maturity	Service oriented, dedicated, team perspective, experience	Adaptability, techno-literacy, independence, willing to buck system	Collective action, optimism, techno-savvy	Most diverse generation in US history
Motivations	Overall good of organization, experience is respected	Being valued and needed, live to work	Permission to work on own schedule, their way without constraints of rules, job mobility, flexibility, work to live	Personal career goals, expectation of promotion, working with other bright and creative people, switch career paths frequently	Structure and stability, changing jobs constantly, career multitaskers
Preferred method of communication	Written, prefer one-on-one, face-to-face, formal memos	In-person, verbal, personal interaction, teams, meetings	Voicemail, email, direct communication	Instant messages, text messages, emails, social media	Handheld communication devices

Generational Differences (continued)

	Silent Generation	Boomers	Gen X	Millennial	Gen Z
Leadership preferences	Hierarchy	Consensus	Competence	Achievement, pulling together	Inclusive communities and policies
View of authority	Respectful	Impressed	Unimpressed	Relaxed	
Feedback preferences	Doesn't seek feedback, no news is good news	Doesn't appreciate feedback	Will ask for feedback	Wants frequent feedback and asks	
Interactive style		Team player	Free agents	Entrepreneurial	
Attitude toward technology	Adapted, largely disengaged	Acquired, early information technology adapters	Assimilated, digital immigrants	Integral digital natives	Entirely dependent on technology
Attitude toward education	A dream	A birthright	A way to get there	An incredible expense	
Financial priorities	Managing income/ expenses to live within means	Generating enough income to live comfortably	Reducing personal debt	Managing income/ expenses to live within means	

Further Reading

- Dimock M. Defining generations: Where Millennials end and Generation Z begins. Pew Research Center, January 17, 2019. Accessed Jan 10, 2021. https://www.pewresearch.org/fact-tank/2019/01/17/where-millennials-end-and-generation-z-begins/

- Hernaus T, Vokic NP. Work design for different generational cohorts: determining common and idiosyncratic job characteristics. J Organ Chang Manag. 2014;27(4):615–641.

- Peterson D. Four generations: can't we get along? Arthur Maxwell. People, Teams, Organizations. September 2011. Accessed Feb 1, 2021. http://arthur-maxwell.com/articles/2011/09-generations.php

- Purdue University Global. Generational differences in the workplace. Accessed Feb 1, 2021. https://www.purdueglobal.edu/education-partnerships/generational-workforce-differences-infographic/

DIVERSITY AND DEMOGRAPHICS

Mike Chaddock, DVM, EML, and Ken Gorczyca, DVM

"It is not our differences that divide us. It is our inability to recognize, accept, and celebrate those differences."

–Audre Lorde

As you launch your career, prioritizing diversity, inclusion, and equity creates an environment that respects, values, and leverages individual differences. Diversity is not a human resources issue—it is a strategic issue that should be reflected throughout the mission, vision, and values of an organization. Success requires that all three, diversity, inclusion, and equity, be implemented. In many cases, a fundamental change in the attitudes and behaviors of an organization's leadership may be needed. You can be that change agent that assures your success, guides your outlook on life, helps others, and fosters personal happiness.

An open, diverse, inclusive, and equitable workforce increases cross-fertilization of ideas and solutions, employee morale, productivity, and competitive advantages. Individuals who work in such environments usually perform better and bring their authentic self to the workplace; thus, the organization receives the best possible results from its workforce.

Diversity

Diversity includes all the ways people are different and unique: age, gender, race, ethnicity, national origin, religion, ability/disability, sexual orientation, gender identity and expression, marital status, socioeconomic status, education, language, physical appearance, thought, ideas, perspectives, and values. Diversity brings the varied perspectives and approaches of different identity groups to a practice or other organization. "Difference" is a source of increased effectiveness and should be integrated into the very core of an organization's culture. The cardinal limitation to improved performance is the leadership's willingness to integrate the experience and approaches of a diversified workforce.

Inclusion

Inclusive environments are those in which any individual or group can fully participate and grow, and be welcomed, respected, supported, leveraged, and valued. Open and explicit discussions are solicited as to how differences can be used as a source of individual and organizational effectiveness. Inclusion encourages and allows for the basics of an organization (functions, strategies, operations, practices, procedures, etc) to be challenged, and it captures the richness of diverse ideas, backgrounds, and perspectives to create business value.

Equity

Equity is the process and procedures that an organization consistently engages in for the fair and just treatment, access, opportunity, and advancement for all people. It means holding people of differing needs to a single expectation and giving them what they need to achieve it. In other words, it is a way to level the playing field.

Privilege

Understanding what privilege is and how it is conveyed can open further avenues for respecting people and their differences. Privilege is when some individuals receive advantages in life solely based on being a member of a particular identity group, either by birth or on a conditional basis. Privilege, by definition, is given and not earned. Privilege occurs when one group's culture, values, or ways of interpreting the world are built into the fabric of institutions within a society and become invisible. The privileged group is commonly treated as the baseline against which others are judged or compared—it is seen as "ordinary," "normal," or "standard."

Having privilege does not mean that individuals are immune to life's hardships, but rather that they benefit from society by nature of their identity. Being privileged also doesn't mean that someone is inherently immoral or undeserving of their achievements. Just because we don't have one kind of privilege doesn't mean that we don't benefit from another. Acknowledging, critiquing, and accepting one's own privilege is not easy. Reflect on, acknowledge, and accept the privileges you have, as well as those you don't have. Force privilege into view, discuss it openly, recognize inequity, and choose to act to change the system of oppression that affords those privileges.

Racial Observations

Racial observations deserve particular attention. The racial make-up of modern American society has shifted dramatically in the past 50 years from white European to black, brown, and Asian (BBA), with some communities 40% or more BBA. Practices and other organizations should strive to reflect the community profile in its staffing and clientele. This is good for business and good for non-BBA staff. In the case of Hispanic staff, an unanticipated benefit may be realized in communicating with Spanish-speaking clients. Encourage advancement for all, including higher education for self-development, and create incentives to do so.

How to Identify Culturally Diverse and LGBTQ (Lesbian, Gay, Bisexual, Transgender, or Queer) Friendly Educational and Employment Opportunities

Can an employee be fired for simply being gay? In 29 states, this was the case until just recently. Only four states prohibit discrimination based on sexual orientation alone, and 17 states prohibit discrimination based on sexual orientation and gender identity. Many of the 29 states that do not have any state-wide prohibited discrimination protection may have city, municipality, or township ordinances prohibiting discrimination.

Inclusiveness is beneficial to all employees in a practice or members of a particular community. Discrimination against LGBTQ employees has negative consequences for worker mental and physical health. An atmosphere of exclusivity legitimizes other forms of prejudice and discrimination. LGBTQ-supportive policies improve community climate. "Closeted" LGBTQ employees report significantly greater dissatisfaction with their rates of promotion and advancement. In addition, they are 40% less likely to trust their employer, and 73% more likely to leave their companies within the next 3 years. Being "in the closet" at work—when you feel unable to be openly LGBTQ with all your colleagues—is not usually much fun. You have to invent facts to cover realities. You watch how you present, what you say, who is watching.

When seeking a place of employment, externship, residency, or graduate education, remember you are interviewing and assessing your potential employer or educational setting as much as they are interviewing you. LGBTQ-friendly offices or educational institutions will have an inclusive non-discrimination policy clearly posted with a zero tolerance in effect 24/7 on the premises; employee sensitivity training for LGBTQ issues, including gender identity and expression; domestic partner benefits; and markets to and engages in appropriate and respectful advertising or sponsorships in the LGBTQ community. Most importantly, you will want to assess if the head of the organization (eg, practice owner, CEO, dean, university president) is actively committed to an LGBTQ supportive environment.

Be sure to carefully read the employee or student handbook and the non-discrimination policy. Does the policy clearly address both sexual orientation and gender identity, or are generic anti-harassment or other corporate statements vague and non-inclusive? As you are evaluating your possible place of employment or education, consider the following: Are there all-gender bathrooms? On forms for employees, students, and/or clients, is there a blank space after the question of gender so people can identify how they want? Is gender-neutral language (eg, partner) used? Is there a highly visible diversity/inclusion/equity image and narrative on the organization's web site that acknowledges self-identified personal gender and use of gender-neutral pronouns?

The LGBTQ Population in the United States

In looking forward toward your career, it might be helpful to know a few demographic statistics. From observations and surveys, Americans are becoming more accepting in their views of LGBTQ people and homosexuality in general, and the number of people identifying as LGBTQ has grown in recent years. Approximately 4.3% of adults in the United States identify as LGBTQ (there is no consensus about how best to measure sexual orientation).

There are demographic differences in who identifies as LGBTQ. The most notable is by age. Young adults, ages 18–36, are by far the most likely to identify as LGBTQ. Gay men and lesbians are more likely than bisexuals to be "out." That means that there are more than 10.7 million LGBTQ adults in the United States. A recent Williams Institute Report estimates that 1.4 million adults (0.6% of adults) in the United States identify as transgender. Roughly half of the LGBTQ population identify as bisexual.

While the prevalence of marriage in the general population continues to decline, the number of same-sex married couples has increased significantly in the last decade as LGBTQ people gained the freedom to marry nationwide. Nearly 1.1 million LGBTQ people in the United States are married to someone of the same sex. That means there are more than 547,000 married same-sex couples nationwide. According to a 2015 Gallup Poll, over 1.2 million LGBTQ people in the United States are in an unmarried same-sex relationship. Given that this poll was conducted before nationwide marriage equality, some of these couples may have married since gaining the legal right to do so.

The Gallup Daily tracking survey asked the following question of people living in the United States: "Do you personally identify as lesbian, gay, bisexual, or transgender?" The following data points include all individuals who self-identified as LGBTQ (both single and coupled).

Population: LGBTQ individuals are 4.5% of the population, with a gender ratio of 42% male and 58% female.

Race/ethnicity: 58% identified as being white, 21% as Latino/Latina, 12% as black, and 5% as more than one race/ethnicity.

Average age: 37.3 years for LGBTQ individuals (47.9 for non-LGBTQ individuals)

Unemployed: 9% of LGBTQ individuals (5% of non-LGBTQ individuals)

Uninsured: 15% of LGBTQ individuals (12% of non-LGBTQ individuals)

Food insecure: 27% of LGBTQ individuals (15% of non-LGBTQ individuals)

Income less than $24,000: 25% of LGBTQ individuals (18% of non-LGBTQ individuals)

The highest percentage of LGBTQ population in the United States is the District of Columbia at 9.8%, followed by Oregon, Nevada, Massachusetts, California, Washington, and Vermont (ranging from 5.2% to 5.6%). The seven states with the lowest LGBTQ population percentage are Kansas, Arkansas, Alabama, South

Dakota, Montana Idaho, and North Dakota (ranging from 3.3% to 2.7%).

In the United States, 70% of LGBTQ adults own pets, while 63% of heterosexual adults own pets. The same poll shows that 90% of gay pet owners say their pet is a member of their family, and two-thirds have bought their pets presents for the holidays. LGBTQ pet owners are slightly more likely than heterosexual pet owners to have cats (63% versus 52%). However, the inverse was found with dogs, with 71% of straight pet owners having a dog versus 63% of LGBTQ pet owners having a dog.

Final Thoughts

When considering employment for your first veterinary position, moving to another job, or working to improve a current environment, use your intuition, keep an open mind, ask questions, discuss, value others' opinions, and look inward to evaluate your own perspectives and biases. Today there are many online resources for the LGBTQ veterinary medical community, such as PrideVMC.org.

We can all effect positive change in ourselves and our communities. Each of us has an important role in recognizing differences among our colleagues and organizations, using tolerance and respect, providing opportunities to others to achieve their personal success, and working for the common good.

Further Reading

- Barron LG, Hrebl MR. Extending lesbian, gay, bisexual and transgender supportive organizational policies: communities matter too. *Ind Organ Psychol.* 2010;3(1):79–81.

- Bolger M. What's the difference between diversity, inclusion, and equity?" Accessed Jan 11, 2021. https://generalassemb.ly/blog/diversity-inclusion-equity-differences-in-meaning/

- Cogan J. *Examining the Employment Nondiscrimination Act (ENDA): The Scientists' Perspective.* American Psychological Association; 2011.

- Irving D. *Waking Up White and Finding Myself in the Story of Race.* Elephant Room Press; 2014:207.

- Jordon H. Moving from diversity to inclusion. *Profiles in Diversity Journal.* March 21, 2011.

- Kapila M, Hines E, Searby M; Proinspire. Why diversity, equity, and inclusion matter. Oct 6, 2016. Accessed Jan 11, 2021. http://independentsector.org/resource/why-diversity-equity-and-inclusion-matter/

- King EB, Cortina JM. The social and economic imperative of lesbian, gay, bisexual, and transgendered supportive organizational policies. *Ind Organ Psychol.* 2010;3(1):69–78.

- LGBT Demographic Data Interactive, January 2019, Los Angeles, CA, The Williams Institute, UCLA School of Law.

- Municipal Equality Index 2020. Human Rights Campaign. Accessed Jan 11, 2021. https://www.hrc.org/resources/municipal-equality-index

- Pride Veterinary Medical Community. http://PrideVMC.org

- Sample Equal Employment Opportunity Policies. HRC Foundation, 2012. Accessed Jan 11, 2021. http://www.hrc.org/resources/entry/sample-equal-employment-opportunity-policies

DRIVING FORCES IN THE VETERINARY PROFESSION

Michael Dicks, PhD, and Melissa Maddux, DVM

"To succeed, you need to find something to hold on to, something to motivate you, something to inspire you."

–Tony Dorsett

The path to becoming a veterinarian is a long climb. As you progress through school, working your way through the challenges of the veterinary educational mountain, you should also begin to prepare yourself for the challenges you will confront in your career as an individual veterinarian and as a member of the veterinary profession. Significant challenges include the following:

- High levels of educational debt
- The gap between the veterinary care that animals need and the care they receive
- The implications of changing demographics of the profession on the availability and desires of veterinary service providers
- The change in veterinary practice ownership from entrepreneurial, independent practices to practice management/corporate groups

Although the veterinary profession has always faced challenges, perhaps no recent period has posed such a unique combination of issues that have conspired to constrain the ability of individual practitioners to control their own professional destinies. The ability to control the type of care, for the type of animals, and in the geographic location you would prefer will not just happen on its own. You must choose to make it happen, and that should begin now.

A veterinary education trains you to apply a problem-solving process to every patient by taking the history, performing a physical examination, running diagnostic tests, developing a treatment plan, and confirming the desired result. This problem-solving process is as critical for your personal, financial, and professional well-being as it is for animal care. Applying the same rigorous process to the major challenges of the veterinary profession will allow you to create and develop both a fulfilling professional career and a satisfying lifestyle.

Managing Debt and Earning Income

Upon graduation, you will have absorbed more veterinary knowledge and have a keener appreciation for the profession than those in any previous generation. However, meeting the challenge of high educational debt will likely fall outside the curriculum of most veterinary colleges. Substantial debt requires a well-defined plan to manage repayment while having a lifestyle that meets your personal expectations. On one end of the spectrum, 17% of new graduates have no debt, while on the other end, more than 50% of new graduates have educational debt that is greater than twice their starting income. For most, an income-based repayment plan will be needed to repay the loan. Unfortunately, income-based repayment plans often result in a loan payoff amount that increases every year and can become a source of stress and anxiety.

Although dealing with the debt that accumulated during veterinary school will be a burden, the real issue will be to earn sufficient income while practicing the type and amount of veterinary medicine that you choose while having a meaningful and rewarding life. Most importantly, this challenge is not isolated but rather intricately woven within the constraints that may be imposed by an employer. Will your future employer encourage you to practice veterinary medicine in the manner that you are excited about, or will they be focused only on maximizing economic return?

Professional and Personal Goals

Our satisfaction in life is determined by our approach to the opportunities before us and the decisions we make. Perhaps not since the decline in the importance of the horse in the early 20th century have new veterinarians faced this degree of challenge in redefining and characterizing the veterinary profession.

Roughly two out of three new graduates will work in a companion animal practice. The recent expansion of corporate investment in veterinary practices means that most new graduates will work for a shareholder-owned corporation. In general, the principal goal of corporate practices is financial performance, while most practices owned by veterinarians prioritize animal health and client relationships. While these goals are not mutually exclusive, their pursuit is not often practiced simultaneously in most veterinary hospitals.

Optimal financial performance in veterinary practice is crucial in managing educational debt while supporting a desired lifestyle. However, striving for increasing fiscal performance at the expense of animal health and client relationships will adversely impact personal well-being, the integrity of the veterinarian-client relationship, and the role of the veterinarian in animal health.

The challenges of managing debt, closing the gap between the veterinary care needs of animals and the current levels of care received, and practicing veterinary medicine in a manner that is professionally and personally rewarding may seem as distant as foreign countries not yet visited. But unlike those foreign countries, these challenges will be there to confront you at the end of your veterinary education. If you are comfortable waking up in a new country without knowledge of the culture, geography, or language, then you will be okay at graduation. However, if the idea of waking up in a position of having little or no information on what to do or how to do it, then you're going to want to look beyond veterinary classes to prepare yourself for work and life after graduation.

Choices

The choices you make will have a lasting impact on both your professional life and your personal lifestyle. As you make these decisions, you should consider the following factors:

- the amount of time you want to devote to your profession (the number of hours a week you want to work, the number of weeks off you want for vacation, etc)
- the location and type of community you want to live in
- the role you want to have in your community, both as a veterinary professional and as a community member
- the type of household that you envision (single, married, children, surrounded by animals)
- perhaps most importantly, the relative value you place on each of these choices

Recognizing your professional ambitions and the financial resources you'll need for the lifestyle you want, while considering the impact of educational debt means that you will have to confront some difficult decisions about expenditures during school and your career pathway. To find the best path will require more than the technical knowledge you will acquire in veterinary school. No two paths will be the same as you customize a plan for your particular situation and goals looking toward the future.

Income earned through the practice of veterinary medicine may not be sufficient to meet the needs of your personal lifestyle and pay students loans either now or in the future. However, leveraging your current income in investments may increase future earnings.

Examples of leveraged investments include acquiring board certification, owning a home, or making other capital investments.

Practice ownership is one such capital investment that will allow you to increase your annual earnings, accumulate wealth, practice veterinary medicine the way you think best, and live where you want. The sooner you become an owner, the greater the impact on lifetime earnings and wealth accumulation. If you don't aspire to own and manage a practice (or have some role in practice management), you will need to recruit a good manager—someone who, with you as the chief medical officer, can be trusted to handle the necessary business tasks for the practice to run smoothly and efficiently.

Over the last decade, practice owners have struggled to sell their hospitals to individuals because many younger veterinarians are unable or unwilling to purchase practices. As a result, corporate entities and practice management groups (consolidators) have been filling the gap. Today, 20% of veterinary practices provide over 50% of companion animal veterinary services, and 60% of these practices are owned by corporations or practice management groups. But there are still nearly 20,000 independent companion animal practices, many with considerable growth potential, and as many as half of these will be for sale in the next 10 years. You may want to consider investigating an arrangement to build equity (eg, work to own) in the practice for when the current owner retires.

Finding Your Path

Individuals and organizations throughout the profession are working to lower the cost of veterinary education, simplify educational debt repayment, and assist new graduates in becoming practice owners. Reach out to them, particularly state veterinary medical associations, to see if they can help you meet the challenge of becoming the veterinary professional you want to be. Other sources to help you find the right path may include family members, financial and career counselors, and school advisors. You may be able to find helpful resources and even a business mentor through SCORE, a network of volunteer business mentors dedicated to helping small businesses. Finding the right path to meet both your professional and personal goals will require effort outside of veterinary school and a firm commitment to develop your plan for after graduation.

You will have made it to the top of the mountain if you wake up every day after graduation, stating, "this is the greatest profession" and looking forward to going to work and making a difference in the lives of your patients, clients, colleagues, and family.

Further Reading

- Bain B. Employment, starting salaries, and educational indebtedness of year-2019 graduates of US veterinary medical colleges. *J Am Vet Med Assoc.* 2020;257(3):292–297.

- Bain B, Dicks MR. Are veterinary students accumulating unreasonable amounts of debt? *J Am Vet Med Assoc.* 2016;249(3):285–288.

- Davidow B. The Veterinary Idealist. Thoughts on Ownership, Quality, Sustainability, and Community. Accessed Jan 11, 2021. https://vetidealist.com

- Dicks MR. A short history of veterinary workforce analyses. *J Am Vet Med Assoc.* 2013;242(8):1051–1060.

- Mullins TL. The humble beginnings of the corporate companion animal hospital. *Vet Herit.* 2012;35(2):59–64.

ORGANIZED VETERINARY MEDICINE AND COLLABORATIVE LEADERSHIP

Roger K. Mahr, DVM

"You cannot afford to stand aloof from your professional colleagues in any place. Join their associations, mingle in their meetings, giving of the best of your talents, gathering here, scattering there but everywhere showing that you are at all times faithful students, as willing to teach as to be taught."

–Sir William Osler

Gratitude, Service, and Responsibility

The foundation for my career in veterinary medicine has also been the basis for my outlook on life. It can be summarized in three words: gratitude, service, and responsibility. These are all linked to organized veterinary medicine, as well as to private practice and the many other roles that veterinarians have in our society.

I am grateful for my roots growing up on a dairy farm and for those life experiences that I had before becoming a doctor of veterinary medicine. I encourage you to think about your past, your achievements, and your significant experiences and to optimize the advantages and opportunities they provide as guiding foundations for your career in veterinary medicine. We can all be justly proud of our rich personal and collective heritage.

As a veterinary student, your first and primary service is to make the most of your educational opportunities. Use all the resources available to you, including your instructors, mentors, and the university environment and facilities, to develop your knowledge and skills. As you begin your career, the tide will shift as your ability and opportunities expand to be of service to others.

Veterinary medicine is a small profession with numerous opportunities and great responsibilities. Our diversity of expertise (eg, private practice, academia, public health, biomedical research), combined with a commitment of working together, defines our profession. No other profession, I believe, has a comparable value to society or has as much impact on the health of both animals and people.

Organized Veterinary Medicine

The American Veterinary Medical Association (AVMA) is the unifying voice of our profession. It was founded in 1863 as the United States Veterinary Medical Association (USVMA). Although the stated purpose and objectives of the AVMA have changed over the course of history, including its name in 1898, the concept of the advancement of veterinary education and science to improve the practice of veterinary medicine for the benefit of both animals and society has been a consistent objective since its origin.

Organized veterinary medicine at the local level began even before the USVMA. Local associations were often established in relationship with the early veterinary colleges, focusing on education and on conveying new knowledge to veterinary practitioners. The establishment of state veterinary associations soon followed as concern heightened for needed state legislation to regulate the practice of veterinary medicine for two primary purposes: to prevent and control the spread of animal diseases and to preserve the status of the qualified graduate veterinarian.

The current organizational structure of the AVMA includes the Board of Directors, House of Delegates, and numerous councils, committees, task forces, and working groups. A dedicated AVMA staff provides administrative oversight and support for these various entities, but it is the member veterinarians who are the heart of the AVMA. Member volunteers provide their expertise and input to develop resources, guiding policies, and educational tools for our profession on a vast array of important issues, including federal and state advocacy, veterinary workforce and education, veterinary economics, public health, animal welfare, disaster response, antimicrobial resistance, scope of practice, telemedicine, diversity, equity and inclusion, and personal well-being. Member volunteers serve individually and collectively to drive and lead the activities of the AVMA in all these areas to ensure the strength and direction of the veterinary profession toward positive change.

The critical issues of the veterinary profession touch our lives every day, whether experienced veterinarian, recent graduate, or student. The Student American Veterinary Medical Association (SAVMA), the national organization of veterinary students, was established by the AVMA in 1969. SAVMA is one avenue for veterinary students to develop their leadership skills and experience organized veterinary medicine on a national level. Students serve on several AVMA committees, and SAVMA is represented as a voting member within the AVMA House of Delegates. If you have not already done so, I strongly encourage you to become an active member of SAVMA, as well as other professional organizations that provide student membership and are of special interest to you. Lifelong friendships and relationships built now through student association and later professional involvement in organizational activities will also provide an unlimited source of knowledge along with professional strength, personal camaraderie, and overall satisfaction throughout your career.

Collaborative Leadership

Each local, state, national, or species-specific veterinary organization possesses a commitment to address those issues of greatest priority to achieve its respective mission. This calls for visionary leadership from within its membership along with communication, coordination, and collaboration to establish a viable strategic planning process. Through this process, a shared vision is developed, and actions to achieve that vision are identified and implemented. This commitment of collaborative leadership ensures the future of our profession and empowers us to provide servant leadership throughout our professional career to best serve society.

During my tenure as AVMA president, my sense of responsibility to the future was highlighted by an initiative for One Health. Of particular significance was the National Academy of Sciences study, "Animal Health at the Crossroads: Preventing, Detecting, and Diagnosing Animal Diseases." The overriding recommendations from this study focused on improving communication, coordination, and collaboration among professional associations, academia, government agencies, nongovernmental organizations, and industry. This study emphasized that we are living in a changing environment, populated by interconnected animal and human contact. This convergence of people, domestic animals, wildlife, and the environment creates complex challenges. These One Health challenges require integrated solutions and call for collaborative leadership. Recognizing this call, I was fortunate to develop a most rewarding personal and professional relationship with the late Dr. Ronald Davis. Dr. Davis was a preventive medicine physician—and the first public health physician to ever serve as president of the American Medical Association (AMA). Through our respective leadership roles, we were able to achieve a collaborative relationship between the AVMA and AMA that allowed us to articulate a collective vision for One Health around the world.

In April 2007, the AVMA Executive Board established the One Health Initiative and formed the AVMA One Health Initiative Task Force. In June 2007, under the leadership of Dr. Davis, a One Health resolution was unanimously approved by the AMA House of Delegates, which called for the AMA to engage in a dialogue with the AVMA to discuss means of enhancing collaboration in medical education, clinical care, public health, and biomedical research.

I share this summary of the origin of the One Health Initiative to illustrate the value of assuming our professional responsibilities, both as individuals and as organizations, as we look toward the future. In addition, the One Health Initiative demonstrates the impact of collaborative leadership to create bold initiatives of action to bring about positive change. It is imperative for veterinarians to collaborate with colleagues in human medicine, public health, bioengineering, animal and human sciences, environmental and social sciences, and other health science–related disciplines. We can accomplish more to improve health worldwide together than we can alone, and the veterinary medical profession can and should continue to assume a major leadership role in that effort.

Future Leaders

The scope of the veterinary medical profession encompasses an extensive range of professional activities with specific vocational interests, including companion animal, equine, bovine and other ruminants, swine, avian, food safety and public health, laboratory animal, and many others. Organizations of veterinarians represent, lead, and support the advancement and advocacy for these specific areas of our profession. The diversity of our activities and the unity of our profession are both great strengths, and you are our future leaders. By joining with your veterinary colleagues, you can help shape the future of our profession. Your voice, support, and leadership are needed to address the important issues that we face. I challenge you to reflect, periodically throughout your career, on your responsibility as a member of the veterinary medical profession and to act upon it.

Further Reading

- American Veterinary Medical Association. https://www.avma.org

- American Veterinary Medical Association. *The AVMA: 150 years of education, science, & service.* American Veterinary Medical Association; 2012.

- American Veterinary Medical Association. *One Health: A New Professional Imperative.* One Health Initiative Task Force: Final Report; 2008. Available at https://www.avma.org/resources-tools/reports/one-health-ohitf-final-report-2008

- National Research Council. *Animal Health At The Crossroads: Preventing, Detecting, and Diagnosing Animal Diseases.* National Academies Press; 2005.

- Smithcors JF. *The American Veterinary Profession Its Background and Development.* Iowa State University Press; 1963.

A VETERINARY EDUCATION AND CAREER

VETERINARY COLLEGE

Lonnie J. King, DVM, MS, MPA, DACVPM

"An investment in knowledge pays the best interest."

–Benjamin Franklin

For many, the life of a veterinary medical student is a 4-year blur of requirements and activities, courses and labs, endless pages of notes and class work, and, of course, tests. We seem to tolerate the accompanying sacrificial sleep deprivation and believe that it is a necessary means to an end. While this description of your college experience may be realistic, it is helpful to understand and appreciate that 4 years of veterinary education has an important purpose and overarching goal. It is designed to help you build a lifelong professional foundation for your future success and to lead you through a remarkable personal transformation.

Although not always apparent, a veterinary education has been thoughtfully planned; through its curricula, experiential learning, and building of clinical and personal competencies, it will enable you to be exposed to the many facets of the veterinary profession. In addition, veterinary colleges must meet accreditation standards, ensure that you have entry-level competencies, and help prepare you to pass the national and state boards needed to engage in private practice.

The Grand Plan of a Veterinary Education

A veterinary medical education has been designed to enable you to do the following:

- acquire a strong basic science foundation and have opportunities to apply this knowledge
- attain excellent medical and surgical skills
- think critically and understand and use research methodologies
- make evidence-based decisions and sound clinical judgments
- adopt lifelong learning for professional growth
- understand and implement primary care principles and techniques
- cultivate an interest in ethics and animal welfare
- have an appreciation for and knowledge of global health, public health, and One Health, including knowledge of wildlife, zoo animals, and fish
- enhance competencies in nontechnical and interpersonal skills
- appreciate diversity and cultural differences
- understand the limits of your knowledge and have the skills and ability to address those limitations

A veterinary medical education also is a time of critical and formative transitions. First, there is the transition from an undergraduate to a professional student; then from acquiring more basic science and medical knowledge to the clinical application of this knowledge and development of new skills; and finally, from a veterinary student to a graduate veterinarian with day-1 competencies. Thus, veterinary school shouldn't be just a blur to you, but rather a confluence of science, clinics, knowledge, skills—a formation of an identity that will transform you both professionally and personally. It will open new vistas of the many possibilities and options available to you to improve the lives of people and animals and to sustain the environment. Instead of a means to an end, consider veterinary school as a fundamental life reset.

Educational Goals in Response to Society

Societal needs have influenced the veterinary profession and driven educational goals throughout our history. The relationship between animals and people has been recorded for millennia but was especially noteworthy beginning in Medieval Europe along with significant advances in the medical sciences. Veterinary medical education was launched during this time and can be traced back to two driving forces: 1) the need for better equine health and medicine because horses were important for military superiority, and 2) the high costs of recurring animal epidemics with unprecedented mortality rates. Cattle plague, later known as rinderpest, and glanders in horses were particularly significant diseases that had great public impact.

In response to these concerns, the first veterinary college was created in 1761 in Lyon, France. The 19th century was characterized by the opening of other veterinary medical educational institutions across Europe. Louis Pasteur and Robert Koch were instrumental in establishing the science of microbiology and advances in comparative medicine with their studies on animal diseases. In the United States, as our population increased, there was a growing demand for more food, and the US livestock industries flourished along with the increasing value of food animals. The growth in the demand for more food and more food animals, along with the creation of the land grant university system in 1862, led to the opening of more US colleges of veterinary medicine, beginning with the first public veterinary medical college at Iowa State University in 1879.

Veterinary medical education continued to evolve, and the next major transition was driven by societal demands for more companion animals with the recognition of the human-animal bond and improved animal welfare. Medical specializations expanded to include more internships, residencies, and specialty boards. New specialties continue to emerge and evolve today as society expects and demands more of the veterinary profession. In addition, new emphases and needs have arisen in public health, ecosystem management, food safety and security, biomedical research, and global health. This expansion of the scope and scale of the profession has led to the adoption of a One Health strategy by many veterinary educational programs. One Health is the concept and approach that addresses complex challenges to promote the health and well-being of all species, including people, and the environment through integration of relevant sciences at the systems level.

Since the opening of the first veterinary college, the most serious challenge to our profession and veterinary educators continues to be meeting societal needs. A report on workforce needs in veterinary medicine from the National Academy of Sciences indicates that *"Our rapidly changing and interdependent world has created remarkable opportunities for the profession to be more relevant than at any other time in history. The action is clear: the profession must proclaim and demonstrate its relevance to the public and to decision-makers to ensure its future success."* As a veterinary student or new graduate, you are living in a propitious and unprecedented time full of opportunity and possibilities but also of increasing responsibilities and obligations. Success is not going to be based on opportunities available to you, because there are more than at any time in history, but rather on your ability to develop the critical competencies to tackle these opportunities.

Educational and Personal Growth
Veterinary medical education continues to change and evolve but at a pace never previously experienced. Technology has been

especially responsible for this unparalleled pace of change. Human knowledge has already transitioned from linear to exponential growth. Today, it is estimated that human knowledge is doubling every 13 months. This has led to an emphasis on how to learn and relearn in the future rather than on trying to memorize more material. Veterinary colleges are designing and adopting competency-based educational outcomes and promoting active learning and self-learning processes. Your veterinary education is progressively based on ensuring your success as a veterinarian working in our complex world and not just on your success as a veterinary student. As a result, you are being prepared to master core principles, think critically and solve complex problems, work collaboratively, communicate well, commit to self-learning and improvement, and maintain an intellectual curiosity and life of inquiry throughout your career.

A useful activity while in school is to establish a self-directed map to ensure your growth and development of critical skills. This type of exercise will make your time at school more relevant, focused, and constructive, and can be accomplished through the following steps:

1. Envision your ideal self or the person you wish to become.
2. Evaluate your real self—the person you are today, along with your strengths and weaknesses.
3. Identify the gaps between 1 and 2, and then create a learning agenda to fill the gaps.
4. Master new behaviors and take on new roles and experiences.
5. Develop supportive and trusting relationships to make change possible and ensure that your plan becomes a reality.

Another important change in veterinary education is a new, and timely, emphasis on your well-being. Living in a rapidly changing and electronic world is difficult and is often magnified by unrealistic expectations, pressure, and the need for perfectionism. There is no question that trying to maintain a balance between well-being and the stresses of school, life, and a job is especially challenging. However, one can be neither successful nor fulfilled without learning to be resilient and emotionally healthy. Veterinary school is about supporting and helping each other; the days of academic competition are over, and one graduates as part of a class. Plan to take time out on occasion to build your personal capacity and resiliency through renewing your physical, mental, social/emotional, and spiritual dimensions and maintain a balance among these during school and throughout your professional life. Great veterinarians and leaders always acknowledge their fallibility; however, they also view them as exceptional learning experiences.

Veterinary school will result in forming lifelong friendships, finding helpful mentors, and establishing professional habits. Your student days will be a combination of good days and bad days, just like they will be in private practice or another career path. You should take advantage of the opportunity to join school clubs and other organizations and to participate in the many remarkable experiences offered during your education. This will open the entire world of veterinary medicine to you, including global health opportunities.

Veterinary medicine is a science but also an art, consisting of a lifetime of learning experiences leading to continual improvement. When the famous cellist Pablo Casals was asked why he continued to practice late in life, he stated that he thought he was finally making some good progress. Your life will continue to transform from knowledge and fact to true wisdom and a healthy respect for things beyond your control. Remember that you and your classmates will graduate as the best prepared veterinarians compared with any class that has come before you.

Beyond Your Four Years

I wish to share a final and inspirational thought with you. Upon completion of your veterinary medical education and due to your exceptionally hard work, I believe that a special gift awaits. You will now have the foundation to serve society as few others can. Through your next 100,000 hours that represent your life's work time, you will be able to profoundly improve the lives and health of animals and people for the next 3, 4, or even 5 decades.

The faculty and staff of your colleges and schools work especially hard and are dedicated to help prepare you for your lifelong careers. The 4 years of a veterinary medical education are not just a blur to an end but rather the groundwork to launch you into a life of immense purpose and passion, indeed a life worth living each day. Step back and think how you might best spend your time during your 4 years of veterinary education and then imagine who you can become and what you can achieve. Veterinary school may very well be the most important time in your life—foundational, transformative, and life-changing.

Further Reading

- Dunlop RH, Williams DJ. *Veterinary Medicine: An Illustrated History.* Mosby; 1996.

- Hart J. Information explosion and information half-life. *Modern Workplace Learning 2020: Building a continuous learning culture.* Accessed Feb 22, 2020. https://www.modernworkplacelearning.com/cild/

- National Research Council. *Workforce Needs in Veterinary Medicine.* National Academies Press; 2013.

- Schwabe CW. *Veterinary Medicine and Human Health,* 3rd ed. Williams and Wilkins; 1984.

PRIVATE PRACTICE

Jerry M. Owens, DVM, DACVR

"While the journey seems long and hard at the beginning, with perseverance and dedication the rewards at the end last a lifetime."

–William R. Francis

Most veterinary students have a specific practice type in mind when they embark on their veterinary education. However, interests often change while in school when working with other species or learning about a specialty area. Within a year or two after graduation, many veterinarians consider switching to other practices or venues of service. So, it's important to keep an open mind and your options flexible.

Practice in the 1900s

Before 1925, most veterinarians worked with horses because of the importance of this species in transportation and work (eg, pulling plows, wagons, or carriages). Other practitioners took care of food animals, while few worked exclusively on companion animals. Although mixed animal practitioners in rural communities treated dogs and cats, their services were usually minimal and empirical.

With the development of the gasoline engine and the introduction of tractors, trucks, and automobiles, equine practices began to wane. By 1930, family farms were being sold and urban sprawl was on the rise, with small towns becoming larger towns. In response to this demographic change and because dogs and cats were starting to be considered more as family members, the need for companion animal practitioners increased. To meet this new demand, veterinary schools began teaching more courses in small animal medicine. Also, clinical research studies became more common, and veterinary medicine became more evidenced based. A benchmark of this transition was that veterinary colleges shifted primary anatomical studies from the horse to the dog in the immediate years after World War II.

In the latter half of the 20th century, veterinary education continued to expand, and postgraduate programs and residencies in many clinical specialties and disciplines evolved. Graduates started to choose career paths other than private practice, including working in basic and human medical research and for pharmaceutical and medical device companies.

Practice Ownership and Selection

In the last few decades, practice ownership has shifted. In earlier times, many new graduates started their own solo practice or joined an established practice with plans to later "buy out" the previous owner when that individual retired. Starting a practice right after graduation is now rare; few have the financial resources to begin from scratch and build a clientele base in an underserved area. Moreover, large corporations and multihospital practice groups have become a common model, with independent practices less so, especially in urban regions.

Regardless of ownership, each practice has its own unique culture and "personality," an important factor to assess when seeking employment. You'll want to consider if the practice will be a good fit for you. For example, would you prefer a smaller practice with only one or two other veterinarians, or a larger group practice with a correspondingly larger caseload? Do you seem to mesh well with the other veterinarians in the practice? Does the team, including receptionists and veterinary technicians/nurses, work well together? How well is the practice equipped? What type of geographic area (rural, small town, big city) and neighborhood do you prefer? In rural areas, will you be comfortable driving long distances, including during the night and in inclement weather? How does the compensation (salary and benefits) compare to national averages? Is there time allotted for continuing education? What type of hours will you be expected to work? Will you also be asked to cover emergencies, or is there an emergency clinic nearby?

Succeeding in Private Practice Settings

At the start, it is important to find the right match through careful research and insightful interviewing. Once hired, be aware that you are joining an existing organization with its individual characteristics and established modes of operation. If you perceive improvements or changes that could make the practice more efficient, remember that "honey is better than vinegar," and realize that change rarely happens overnight or sometimes not at all. Seniority in some settings is important and needs to be respected. Be sensitive to colleagues and technical and support staff, as well as be flexible in your own expectations. Success goes beyond technical skills and clinical knowledge; it requires being able to work well with people and refine interpersonal skills. If there are interpersonal conflicts, it may take time to work out differences sensitively, fairly, and compassionately.

Importance of Your First Job

That said, the first year in practice is a critical one, because you will often develop habits during that time—habits that can be good or not so good. In other words, you will develop your style of practice and learn many new skill sets beyond the tremendous amount of knowledge you acquired in veterinary school. The lack of clinical experience can be daunting to any new graduate, and the veterinarians you work with on your first job will become crucial mentors.

You'll be learning how to deal with demanding clients, discuss money matters, handle the sensitive situation of euthanasia and grieving clients, and possibly manage some of the business aspects of the practice. As you gain experience in these and many other common practice situations, mentors can be helpful guides as they provide insight into the nuances of practice and the realities of being a veterinary professional.

Practice Types by Species

- Companion or small animal practice is the most common practice type chosen today by graduating veterinarians. Most practices are dog- and cat-friendly, but some are feline-only and others also provide care for birds, other small pets (eg, rabbits, rodents), and reptiles.

- Mixed animal practices are most often in rural or semi-rural communities. Emergency call is often part of the job. Practice demands can include long hours and depend on the number of veterinarians sharing the caseload and emergency duties.

- Equine practices are often associated with racetracks, breeding farms, or owners who train horses for sport such as endurance riding, fox hunting, dressage, and carriage racing.

- Dairy and beef practices most often involve maintaining herd health and, in the case of dairy cattle, managing reproductive programs. Most bovine practices have multiple veterinarians and serve large geographic areas. Larger group practices may be sophisticated, performing procedures such as embryo transfer and individual medical and surgical treatment of valuable animals.

- Swine veterinarians typically work in practice groups or are employed by large hog producers. Swine practice is mainly concerned with herd health, including vaccination protocols, disease prevention, and nutrition.

- Poultry veterinarians typically work for large poultry

corporations that are vertically integrated. Poultry practice concentrates on flock management, including controlling infectious diseases and maintaining soundness and quality of the meat and eggs through flock nutrition and genetics.

- Zoo veterinarians deal with a wide variety of captive and exotic animals but are few because of the low number of positions available. Large zoos typically have an onsite veterinary staff and equipped hospital facilities, while many smaller zoos rely on part-time help from local large and small animal practitioners.

- Exotic animal practice has increased in recent years, with expanded medical knowledge about these species and the development of specialty training. Most exotic animal veterinarians work in large veterinary centers, universities, or specialty practices.

Other Practice Types and Models

- Part-time positions in private practice are available on either a short- or long-term basis and may be a good option for you, depending on your life circumstances.

- Emergency medicine practice has been another area of recent growth in veterinary medicine. Emergency clinics are common in urban and suburban areas and have qualified emergency veterinarians on staff, many of whom are board certified in emergency medicine and critical care.

- Mobile practice, historically the mainstay of large animal medicine, is growing within the small animal sector. Many mobile units are well equipped, including general anesthesia and surgical facilities. Clients with busy schedules, multiple pets, or pets who dislike car travel (eg, cats) appreciate this "house call" approach.

- Relief veterinarians cover for another veterinarian on a short-term basis. This allows the practice to continue to operate as usual while the "regular" veterinarian is out of the office (eg, vacation, conference). Some veterinarians do relief work only, taking care of short-term needs for multiple practices in an area or region. Because relief veterinarians step into different practices with different equipment/capabilities, staff, and clientele—and are often "left on their own"—they must be able to adapt rapidly and function independently. Having at least a few years of solid practice experience is a good plan before contemplating relief work. Presently, veterinarians who are skilled in livestock species are in high demand for relief work.

- Academic practice at universities generally requires specialty board certification or an advanced degree (or working toward the same). Internship and residency are generally required for an academic appointment. However, some universities offer non-tenure-track community practice–type appointments that primarily involve clinical practice along with some 4th-year student rotation teaching responsibilities.

Outlook

The demand for veterinarians in private practice continues to increase. Many veterinarians spend their entire careers in some form of private practice, while others pursue other areas of interest to best use their knowledge and skills. Some return to universities for residencies or specialized training in other disciplines, or even change careers completely and do something unrelated to veterinary medicine.

The variety of private practice options offer numerous and enriching opportunities for service to patients, clients, and society. It is a matter of finding the best fit for you at particular times in your life, even if it takes several tries, to achieve personal satisfaction. According to William Shakespeare, "The world is your oyster."

Further Reading

- AVMA Reports and Statistics. Economic reports. Market Research Data. American Veterinary Medical Association. https://www.avma.org/resources-tools/reports-statistics

- Kogan LR, Hellyer PW, Stewart SM, et al. Recruitment and hiring strategies of private practitioners and implications for practice management training of veterinary students. *J Vet Med Educ.* 2015;42(2):97–106.

- Milani M. The art of private veterinary practice: intellectual communication. *Can Vet J.* 2011;52(8):897–898.

- Milani M. The art of private veterinary practice: seeing both sides of the problem. *Can Vet J.* 2011;52(6):677–678.

- Milani M. The art of private veterinary practice: working with raise-dependent clients. *Can Vet J.* 2007;48(12):1293–1296.

SPECIALIZATION

Danelle Bickett-Weddle, DVM, MPH, PhD, DACVPM

*"Learning is not attained by chance, it must be sought
for with ardor and attended to with diligence."*

–Abigail Adams

In 4 short years, veterinary students are introduced to the many ailments of the furred and feathered, woolly and scaled, as well as the treatments and prevention options aimed at optimizing animal health, public health, and overall wellness. The world of veterinary medicine is vast and far-reaching. During each semester or term, students are introduced to unfamiliar concepts by instructors who have made that aspect of veterinary medicine their focus. Some of those instructors are renowned researchers—veterinarians who have built a career asking questions and uncovering answers that benefit animal and human health. Other instructors are specialists—veterinarians who have dedicated years to the art and science of veterinary medicine, undergone specialized training, and passed a rigorous examination to earn the title of "diplomate."

Look around the room at your classmates. Over there is a future board-certified surgeon. And that one is a future board-certified nutritionist. The one studying the latest journal may discover the cure for the next global pandemic. The one peering through the microscope? You guessed it, future board-certified pathologist. Look in the mirror—your reflection may be that of a future distinguished researcher and/or diplomate.

Opportunities Abound

Entering veterinary school with an idea of what the future might hold is exciting. For those unsure of the next steps, numerous opportunities are available to explore interests and discover new passions. This can be both exciting and overwhelming. Keep an open mind. Try things outside your comfort zone. Spend time with those who inspire you to grow. When you discover your passion, pursue it with your whole heart, and you can accomplish more than you ever thought possible.

If your passion involves additional education, such as a masters or PhD degree, explore options with researchers, program directors, and institutions that align with your objectives. Many veterinary schools have opportunities to work in research laboratories, where you can contribute to scientific discovery, conduct field research, and even pursue a dual degree in another area (eg, education or public health) while in veterinary school. Now is the time to explore, experience, even fail, and get back up with the support of experienced professionals who are passionate about student learning.

If your passion involves a specialty, learn all you can about the requirements and the path to success. The American Board of Veterinary Specialties provides links to the various veterinary specialty colleges in the United States (see Further Reading, below). Capitalize on summer opportunities that allow you to experience an area of specialized veterinary medicine. Many, although not all, specialties require internships followed by residencies. Most are competitive, requiring strong academic performance and experience in the specific area (eg, internal medicine, surgery, emergency and critical care). Design your clinical year not only to meet graduation requirements but also to ensure you have opportunities to obtain experience in your specialty of interest and to develop positive professional relationships with specialists in this area. Ask questions, immerse yourself in the research, challenges, innovations, and technological advances within the specialty. Write out your goals and work hard to achieve them.

As a mixed animal practitioner, a hypothetical Dr. Morris enjoyed the variety of patients, the clients, and the diagnostic challenges. The quest for answers on the difficult cases was so strong that Dr. Morris wanted to delve deeper, run more tests, or, if the patient did not recover, perform a necropsy to solve the mystery. But not all clients could afford surgery or additional tests, plus many were not comfortable with a postmortem examination of their precious pet. This led Dr. Morris to leave clinical practice to pursue a graduate degree and specialization. Intrigued by interpretation of diagnostic test results and histology, Dr. Morris became a board-certified pathologist. This new career direction, working on challenging cases in all animal species from throughout the United States, supporting veterinary practitioners in their search for answers, brings Dr. Morris a great deal of job satisfaction.

Specialization Options

After earning a veterinary degree, many opportunities exist to continue to hone skills, acquire knowledge, and expand your horizons in one or more specialties. The American Veterinary Medical Association (AVMA) currently provides support to the autonomous American Board of Veterinary Specialties (ABVS) in the United States. The ABVS "recognizes and encourages the development of recognized veterinary specialty organizations promoting advanced levels of competency in well-defined areas of study or practice categories to provide the public with exceptional veterinary service."

The ABVS oversees 22 specialty organizations, which include 40 unique specialties. The variety of specialty options mirrors the diversity of the veterinary profession. Specialization opportunities exist in private or public practice for veterinarians with a desire to complete additional training in numerous areas, including the following:

- Species-specific: companion, food, equine, laboratory, exotic, or zoo animals
- Treatment modalities: anesthesia, behavior, dermatology, dentistry, emergency and critical care, internal medicine, nutrition, ophthalmology, pharmacology, sports medicine, surgery, welfare
- Diagnostics: microbiology, pathology, radiology, theriogenology, toxicology
- Preventive medicine for animals and the public

Within each major specialty, internal medicine for instance, additional opportunities exist for more focused and deeper concentration (eg, cardiology, neurology, oncology). There is no limit to the number of specialties a single veterinarian can achieve.

History of Veterinary Specialties

The first three veterinary specialties recognized by the AVMA were the American College of Veterinary Pathology (recognized in 1950), the American College of Veterinary Preventive Medicine (originally known as the American Board of Veterinary Public Health, also recognized in 1950), and the American College of Laboratory Animal Medicine (recognized in 1957). In 1959, the AVMA created the Advisory Board on Veterinary Specialties (renamed in 1992 as the American Board of Veterinary Specialties) to oversee these three specialties and growing interest in creating others.

To illustrate the scope of change in veterinary medicine in the United States, AVMA records show 14,597 veterinarians and 792 new graduates in 1950. Nearly 70 years later, the AVMA reports over 113,000 veterinarians and approximately 3,000 new graduates. The veterinary population has increased 7-fold and so have the numbers of specialty organizations.

Benefits of Specialization

Providing a higher level of care and achieving a personal goal are common reasons why veterinarians pursue board certification. It takes hard work and dedication to accomplish and, for some, intrinsic motivation drives them to develop professionally because they know they are capable. An important benefit of specialization is the increased job opportunities, which often result in a higher salary than that of nonspecialists. Some employers offer special compensation for certain board-certified specialists. The United States Armed Forces offers this benefit for doctors serving our country in their capacity as health professionals. Different branches of the uniformed services need different specialists, which is described on the Army, Air Force, and US Public Health Service websites. Most specialty organizations offer opportunities to network with colleagues, which is another benefit of being board-certified.

Experience Comes in Many Forms

Specialty organizations are varied in their experience requirement to apply for board certification. Knowing your personal learning style and your career and personal goals is crucial when selecting a specialty to pursue.

Some specialties require an internship followed by a residency. In 2019, the American Association of Veterinary Medical Colleges reported 393 intern trainees at 29 veterinary schools and 1,228 resident trainees across 26 veterinary schools. There are additional interns and residents at private veterinary hospitals studying under specialists. Not all interns go on to become residents, and residency programs can be 2- or 3-year programs. In addition to the hands-on experience, specialty boards may have requirements on publications, case reports, presentations, and teaching.

For those interested in achieving specialty status that does not strictly involve internships or residency, several options exist. Some examples include the American Board of Veterinary Practitioners (which has a practitioner path), the American College of Veterinary Microbiology (which has graduate degree paths), and the American College of Veterinary Preventive Medicine (which has an experience path).

In addition to specialization in clinical areas, veterinarians may specialize in other cross-disciplinary fields, earning an additional degree in public health (MPH), business (MBA), law (JD), or even human medicine (MD).

Looking Forward

Over 13,000 veterinarians in the United States have passed a rigorous board examination to achieve specialist status. Many of these specialists also have advanced degrees. Other veterinarians focus solely on research or academia once achieving their masters and/or PhD degree(s).

As the number of veterinarians and the population of animal owners continue to grow, the number of postgraduate-educated and trained specialists and researchers is expected to as well. As technologies evolve to further advance the prevention and treatment of disease, so too will the number and type of research opportunities and specialty colleges.

Advancements in communication technology will also continue to expand, bringing specialists to clients and their animals, further enhancing animal and public health. Solving the next generation's issues will take inquisitive minds, searching for answers, while ensuring job satisfaction and possibly even peer recognition. Educational and specialty opportunities abound for energetic veterinarians willing to tackle these complex issues.

Further Reading

- AVMA American Board of Veterinary Specialties. Accessed Jan 9, 2021. https://www.avma.org/education/veterinary-specialties

- AVMA ABVS Policies and Procedures, September 2018. Accessed Jan 9, 2021. https://www.avma.org/ProfessionalDevelopment/Education/Specialties/Documents/ABVS-Policies-and-Procedures.pdf

- AVMA Market Research Statistics: U.S. veterinarians 2018. Accessed Jan 9, 2021. https://www.avma.org/resources-tools/reports-statistics/market-research-statistics-us-veterinarians-2018

CAREER PROGRESSION AND CHANGE

Heather Case, DVM, MPH, DACVPM, CAE

*"A mind that is stretched by new experiences
can never go back to its old dimensions."*

–Oliver Wendell Holmes, Jr.

Some scholars believe that veterinary medicine likely developed before human medicine. What is certain is that the veterinary profession has served the needs of the public since its beginning. Initially, veterinary roles included caring for livestock, providing food safety and security, and serving as an essential part of the transportation system working as horse doctors. Over the years, the profession has changed to meet changing public needs, often entering arenas in which veterinary medicine was previously considered unlikely to succeed. For example, many of today's graduates may not be aware of the origin of companion animal practice in this country. In the early 20th century when veterinarians found the numbers of horses they so often treated on the decline in the face of the booming automobile industry, companion animal veterinary medicine was not an obvious choice for many within the leadership of veterinary medicine. It was, in fact, a small group of practitioners who recognized and cultivated this practice area. Only after several veterinarians began teaching themselves companion animal medicine and surgery did the veterinary school curriculum follow suit.

Clinical Practice

The majority of veterinary students today enter veterinary school intent on practicing clinical veterinary medicine, with most entering companion animal practice. With multiple options for practice, be it type of species or specialty area, this is an excellent and almost necessary place for most new veterinarians to land after graduation. In fact, many positions beyond clinical practice require previous practice experience. Some veterinarians will remain in clinical practice throughout their careers, while others will find that clinical practice is simply their starting point within the profession.

Because veterinarians are uniquely trained across multiple species and develop highly useful skills in practice, such as gathering information on patients who cannot speak for themselves and making life-saving decisions in a short amount of time, we are excellent candidates for many positions and opportunities outside of clinical practice.

Beyond Clinical Practice

Veterinarians can be found working in government, human and veterinary medical schools and laboratories, undergraduate colleges, veterinary technician programs, and throughout the "veterinary industry," including vaccine and pharmaceutical companies, pet food and feed manufacturing companies, and nearly everything in between. Veterinarians speak on behalf of the veterinary profession with members of Congress, and veterinarians are even serving with NASA to bring the perspective of veterinary medicine to space exploration.

If you speak to enough veterinarians who are working in areas outside clinical practice, you'll soon learn that each one has a distinctive career path unlikely to be replicated by anyone else. However, what is common to all is that an open mind, combined with a willingness to explore opportunities that arise and are of interest (possibly initially as a volunteer), often lead to new and different career roles not previously apparent to veterinarians.

Case Studies

Let me share with you two real-life case studies of what I mean by career change leading to personal fulfillment.

After 13 years, Dr. Michael Chaddock left the mixed animal practice he built from the ground up to work as a technical services veterinarian with a grain company. Pursuing his growing interest in agriculture led to him serving on a state agriculture committee, and ultimately he applied for and became the State Veterinarian for Michigan. After 15 years in that role, Dr. Chaddock was again ready for a career change. He applied and was selected for the AVMA's competitive Congressional Fellowship Program. His background and experience as a State Veterinarian translated easily into policy development and working on Capitol Hill. After yet a few more career adventures along the way, he landed in a senior administrative role in veterinary academia. Each new experience provided Dr. Chaddock with a new skill set that opened doors to new roles within the veterinary profession.

In my own career, after several rewarding years as a predominantly equine veterinarian in a rural mixed animal practice, new opportunities presented that allowed me to explore related and synergistic interests. I returned to my alma mater to do a residency program in preventive medicine and complete a masters of public health degree. An invitation to work in the turkey industry on entry into my residency program, while a bit of a stretch for a "horse" doctor, allowed me to utilize parts of my existing veterinary skill set in a new arena—at the interface between human and animal health. The veterinary profession is the only health profession whose members take an oath to protect public health.

Another unexpected opportunity arose during my residency program shortly after I volunteered to serve on a newly created veterinary disaster response team. Imagine my surprise when Hurricane Katrina made landfall the very week this disaster response team completed our training and became deployable. This unlikely series of events led me to complete my required public health field experience during the 60 days I spent working on the animal issues as a disaster responder in the wake of the hurricane.

This experience eventually led to working full time in not-for-profit, mission-driven organizations. I had the opportunity to turn my interest in veterinary disaster preparedness and response into a full-time job with the American Veterinary Medical Association. Today, I lead another veterinary not-for-profit mission-driven organization, the International Council for Veterinary Assessment.

Many Possible Roles

Veterinarians are uniquely trained to provide many different services to the world. While our primary focus is the care and welfare of animals, we play a crucial role at the interface between human and animal health and in many career paths along the way. Pay attention to what excites you, explore opportunities, have courage, and develop your expertise in areas of interest. You never know where your curiosity will lead you in this most excellent career that is veterinary medicine.

Further Reading

- History of Veterinary Medicine. *Iowa State University Vet.* 1939;2(1):Article 1. Accessed Jan 9, 2021. https://lib.dr.iastate.edu/iowastate_veterinarian/vol2/iss1/1

- Pritt SL, Case HCF. The importance of veterinary career awareness. *J Am Vet Med Assoc.* 2018;252:1200–1204.

- Smith CA. *Career Choices for Veterinarians: Private Practice and Beyond.* 2nd ed. Smith Veterinary Consulting and Publishing; 2011:103–212, 221–228.

- Smith DF. Introduction. In: Smith DF, Isham GK, Maccabe AT, eds. *Pathways to Progress: the Vision and Impact of Members of the Association of American Veterinary Medical Colleges at the Fiftieth Anniversary* (1966–2016). The Donning Company Publishers; 2016: 13–14.

VERSATILE PROFESSION

Candace A. Jacobs, DVM, MPH, DACVPM, CFS

*"To succeed, jump as quickly at opportunities
as you do at conclusions."*

–Benjamin Franklin

Veterinary education is broad-based and, thus, provides a foundation for a variety of career options. Although your education focuses on diagnosis and treatment of animal disease, many job opportunities are available for veterinarians beyond clinical practice. Societal needs in ecosystem management, public health, food safety and security, and biomedical research have made an impact on our profession. These are not new opportunities, but they have not always garnered attention within the veterinary community. Recent efforts such as One Health, which is the integration of multiple disciplines working together on ideal health for animals, people, and the environment, have helped bring these diverse opportunities forward. Veterinarians are uniquely situated to address One Health challenges because of elements provided in our education: critical thinking skills combined with knowledge and application of good scientific methods, evidence-based decision-making, and population-based medical principles.

Awareness of the diversity of career opportunities beyond clinical practice can broaden your possible employment choices and lead to a career equally (or more) satisfying as private practice, while also potentially providing an improved work–life balance. Many nonclinical positions do not require emergency or weekend work and can provide more flexible family-focused schedules. Some nontraditional work may require travel, but this is commonly prescheduled, sometimes flexible, and always enriching. Additionally, there may be opportunities for employer-funded tuition assistance for advanced training and education as well as payment of professional dues. Larger employers, such as some industry, government, and military organizations, can provide excellent benefits, including health care insurance, sick leave, vacation, savings plans, etc.

With the high cost of veterinary education resulting in significant student loan debt, it's worth considering employment with organizations that offer some repayment options. For example, the Public Service Loan Forgiveness Program provides repayment assistance for veterinarians working full time for 10 years in a qualifying public service employer, or the Army Active Duty Health Professions Loan Repayment Program is available for those serving in the military. Various state-funded and other loan repayment programs exist for veterinarians pursuing careers in academia and for those in clinical practice in a government-designated shortage situation.

Academia

With expansion of new veterinary schools and the large percentage of professors in existing established schools nearing retirement eligibility, there is an increasing need for qualified instructors. Responsibilities of veterinary school professors include providing a challenging professional curriculum for aspiring veterinarians. Faculty members also have an opportunity for clinical service and may serve as department heads, provosts, vice presidents, and even chancellors. You might also teach both undergraduate and graduate students in other colleges and universities in animal sciences, basic sciences, agriculture, or other closely related fields.

Veterinarians have held leadership positions in academia, as deans of not only colleges of veterinary medicine, but also of colleges of arts and sciences, agriculture, and public health. Almost all medical schools have veterinarians on staff (often hiding behind other degrees, such as a PhD). Academic careers also provide opportunities for research and for teaching outside the school environment, such as in continuing education at veterinary or other health-related conferences.

Government Positions

The population-based approach to veterinary medicine is a boon for those seeking employment in the public health arena, which includes positions in federal, state, local, and tribal governments, as well as in the military, some teaching jobs, and international assistance work. These are broad employer groups and offer many different opportunities. For example, you will find interesting careers in the federal government civil service, which includes positions with the US Department of Agriculture (Animal Plant Health and Inspection Service [APHIS], Food Safety Inspection Service [FSIS], Risk Management Agency [RMA], and Agricultural Research Service [ARS], among others), the Department of Health and Human Services (Public Health Service [PHS], Food and Drug Administration [FDA], Centers for Disease Control and Prevention [CDC], National Institutes of Health [NIH]), Fish and Wildlife Service, National Marine Fisheries Service, US Agency for International Development [USAID], Veterans Administration [VA], Environmental Protection Agency [EPA], National Science Foundation [NSF], Agency for Toxic Substances and Disease Registry [ATSDR], and more. Federal jobs include positions in fish and wildlife research and/or medicine, food and/or meat inspection, disaster preparedness, and program management. Additional federal positions include epidemiologist, toxicologist, pathologist, microbiologist, virologist, statistical analyst, import/

export inspector, animal welfare inspector, consumer safety officer, international liaison, and even astronaut (no kidding!).

Federal uniformed service jobs worth considering are with the US Army, the US Air Force, and the US Public Health Service Commissioned Corps. These positions are in every state as well as overseas. The US Army Veterinary Corps hires veterinarians for food inspection, disaster relief, biomedical research, as well as to care for pets and horses. You may also serve in the Reserves or National Guard as a part-time officer. Veterinarians in the Air Force are Public Health Officers in the Biomedical Sciences Corps, focusing on disease control and human public health. The US Public Health Service Commissioned Corps provides employment opportunities for health professionals and students as part of the Department of Health and Human Services. These officers are likely to be assigned to the CDC, EPA, FDA, NIH, or agencies outside the Public Health Service on temporary assignment.

State governments commonly have positions for veterinarians in their departments of agriculture, health, environment, and wildlife. Such positions may be regulatory in nature and are involved with policy development, laboratory analysis, field work, or management. Cities and counties hire veterinarians for positions in animal shelters or animal care facility inspection as well as public health. In forensic veterinary medicine, the techniques of forensic science and crime scene processing are applied to circumstances of animal abuse, neglect, cruelty, fighting, and death. Specializing in this area can assist local law enforcement personnel in addressing animal abuse cases and may involve testifying in court.

Industry Positions

Industry jobs can be found with companies that serve the veterinary profession and that work in other fields of science, software, biotechnology, biomedical science, public health, and food safety, security, and welfare. You may see positions in companies that make products or perform services in medications, medical and/or laboratory supplies and equipment, pet foods, human foods, and retail and wholesale food production. Veterinarians can find positions in several areas, including basic and clinical research and development, quality assurance, regulatory affairs, product registration, technical services, environmental services, and sales and marketing.

International Opportunities and Non-Governmental Organizations

You may want to broaden your horizons with international travel or help others in the global community. Such jobs are commonly with government (eg, uniformed services or federal civilian positions) or with educational, religious, industry, and assistance/service organizations. Duties overseas may be wide-ranging and involve clinical veterinary medicine, animal production, educating owners/producers/foreign veterinarians, public health, research, and economics. Search job openings with the following organizations to get a start: Food and Agriculture Organization–Food Security, World Organization for Animal Health (OIE), US Agency for International Development, and the Peace Corps.

Note that competence in a foreign language, eg, French (Africa) or Spanish (Latin America), is most helpful. Non-governmental organizations, both in the United States and abroad (may be volunteer) include Veterinarians Without Borders, Rural Area Veterinary Services, International Veterinarians Dedicated to Animal Health, Christian Veterinary Mission, and EcoHealth Alliance.

A Personal Note

My own career has been public health–focused, and I've worked in small animal and mixed practice, the military, academia, state government, and the food and beverage industry. This series of jobs, all still within the field of veterinary medicine, became my long-term occupation. I view my career not as a ladder but as more of a matrix, moving up, down, and sideways into new fields and areas of interest. One skill I've found particularly useful is applying information learned in one job to situations in a new job. Curiosity and networking have been keystones in my career progression, as well as some courage to take a step into the unknown.

As you contemplate your career options, seek out information on both clinical and nonclinical opportunities from the Internet and the AVMA Career Center, as well as by networking with fellow veterinarians and other professionals. For more nonclinical positions, investigate veterinary associations whose members are not employed in clinical practice, such as the National Association of Federal Veterinarians, American Association of Industry Veterinarians, Association of American Veterinary Medical Colleges, and American Association of Food Safety and Public Health Veterinarians. You might also look at non-veterinary organizations, such as the Institute of Food Technologists, American Public Health Association, American Conference of Governmental Industrial Hygienists, International Association of Food Protection, American Society of Quality, etc.

In addition to Internet research and networking, reach out to recruiters and/or human resources professionals at organizations that you find appealing. Closely examine job descriptions and requirements of positions that spark your interest. Although you may need to acquire some additional training or pursue certification in an allied area, you might be surprised by the plethora of career options available in nonclinical settings with competencies already provided by your veterinary education.

In the current climate of "hyperspecialization," it's important to back up and look at the big picture and think about how all the puzzle pieces fit together. As a veterinarian, you have a broad choice of career options and many opportunities for fulfillment and service.

Further Reading

- AVMA Veterinary Career Center. Accessed Jan 9, 2021. https://www.avma.org/education/veterinary-career-center

VETERINARIAN-CLIENT-PATIENT RELATIONSHIP

RELATIONSHIP SKILLS

Russell W. Currier, DVM, MPH, DACPVM

"Did you ever stop to think that a dog is the only animal that doesn't have to work for a living? A hen has to lay eggs. A cow has to give milk, and a canary has to sing. But a dog makes his living by giving out nothing but love.

You can make more friends in two months by becoming genuinely interested in other people than you can in two years by trying to get others interested in you. Let me repeat that. You can make more friends in two months by becoming interested in other people than you can in two years by trying to get other people interested in you."

–Dale Carnegie

It behooves veterinary professionals to recognize that social skills are equally, if not more important, than technical skills. This is true not only in medicine but also in the business world, and the business literature can provide much guidance.

The late Earl Nightingale, a 20th-century leadership and motivational guru, tells the story of a grocery store manager who got in a dispute with a customer about the pricing of a product (possibly milk). The argument went on for several minutes, with the customer becoming deeply offended and leaving the store without purchase. An assistant to the manager complimented him on winning the argument, but the manager quickly remarked, *"Yeah, I won the argument but lost a customer who will never shop here again."* No winners there. Remember that the only way to get the best of an argument is to avoid it.

Working with People

Client relationships are particularly important. Our attitude toward others often determines their attitude toward us. Taking a positive approach as much as possible will have a positive influence on how others respond to us and on our relationships in general. It's often helpful to find something you like or appreciate about clients, perhaps something about their dog, cat, or horse. Or maybe you can identify something you have in common, such as a favorite sports team or the make/model of their vehicle. Publilius Syrus (85–43 BCE) said, *"We are interested in others when they are interested in us."* People can easily perceive when they are not liked and may become dissatisfied.

These same principles apply to colleagues—and especially staff. Treat staff members as the valued part of the team that they are, and they will respond in kind. Don't condescend, dictate, or berate, and be prompt to admit your own mistakes. Be slow to criticize; if negative feedback is necessary, be sure to offer it in private. In contrast, be lavish with praise and provide it in front of others. Gratitude and expectancy are the best attitudes, while recognizing that we all work interdependently within a practice or other organization. Recognize, too, that although people work for money out of necessity, they will go the extra mile for recognition and praise.

The Veterinarian-Client-Patient Relationship

In veterinary medicine, we have the triad of veterinarian, client, and patient. Patients need to be viewed as special, especially companion animals, including equine friends. Recognizing the animal's positive features, such as a friendly personality or nice hair coat/grooming, regardless of the reason for presentation, is always meaningful to the client.

Sir William Osler, the revered physician of the late 19th and early 20th centuries, observed, *"Kindliness of disposition and gentleness of manners are qualities essential in a practitioner. If they do not exist naturally, they are virtues which must be cultivated if not assured. The rough voice, the hard-sharp answer, and the blunt manner are as much out of place in the [veterinary] ward as 'any lady's boudoir'."* Good communication is built on trusting relationships.

In a recent study of determining the most promising practices to foster physician [in our case, veterinarian] presence and connection with patients [and clients], it boiled down to these five:

- Prepare with intention.
- Listen intently and completely.
- Agree on what matters most.
- Connect with the patient's story [as reflected by the client].
- Explore emotional clues.

For busy clinicians with multiple demands and distractions, these five recommended practices have the potential to facilitate meaningful intentions with clients and maybe even with animal patients. Remember, too, that clients will be watching how you communicate/interact with and handle their animals.

Remember To Be Human

In today's technological, information-based environment, communications are instant through use of the internet, computers, smart phones, and other mobile devices. Relationships with clients and staff are well served by face-to-face encounters (that means keeping the smart phone in your pocket), leaving social media and other venues for more appropriate times. Remember that nobody is more persuasive than a good listener.

Another way to enhance your relationships with clients is by writing a thank-you note or other acknowledgment—handwritten notes sent by mail are especially meaningful. Under challenging circumstances, you may even elect to walk a client out to his or her car. Show you care.

Dr. Bill McCulloch, a dear friend and colleague offers, *"Learning to interact with clients is as important as learning to care for their pets. Dealing with human emotions is often a challenge. It is useful to understand the five stages of grief, which you will need to deal with when the subject of euthanasia comes up, as well as the concept of anticipatory grief. For example, when clients bring in a sick pet, they are often concerned and scared, wondering if the pet has cancer and worrying about the financial cost. Another situation that may arise is displaced anger in the exam room. Here is an anecdote from my clinical years: A client, distraught over his pet's situation and related cost, became irate and angrily started yelling at me, creating an uncomfortable scene. However, the next day, he returned and apologized for his outburst. He said he was very distressed because just before his wife told him that the dog had been sick for several days, she had also told him that their daughter needed expensive orthodontic work, including braces."*

Realize that our attitudes are conveyed not only by the words we say, but also by our tone of voice and body language. More than 90% of our communication is nonverbal. Learn to read tone and body language and remember that you cannot overcome a client's anger with an argument. Listen, acknowledge the client's feelings, and then work to solve the problem.

Keep Learning

Finally, don't hesitate to study self-help books for insightful ideas and time-tested principles. Works of Dale Carnegie (an early 20th-century personal relationships trainer) and Earl Nightingale would be good starters. Their writings and lectures are replete with methods and examples that can inspire and even possibly preserve your mental well-being.

Further Reading

- Carnegie D. *How to Win Friends and Influence People.* Simon & Schuster; 1936.
- Dale Carnegie & Associates, Inc., Levine SR, Crom MA. *The Leader in You.* Simon & Schuster; 1993.
- Nightingale E. *Lead the Field.* Nightingale Conant Corp; 2007.
- Osler W. *The Quotable Osler.* American College of Physicians; 2008.
- Zulman DM, Haverfield MC, Shaw JG, et al. Practices to foster physician presence and connection with patients in the clinical encounter. *JAMA.* 2020;323(1):70–81.

THE HUMAN-ANIMAL BOND

Sara Mark, DVM

"A dog doesn't care if you're rich or poor,
educated or illiterate, clever or dull.
Give him your heart and he will give you his."

–John Grogan

Undeniably, people and the animals within our world share a bond. For some people, their interest in animals is curious observation, while others have a deep emotional connection. These beliefs are on a continuum, and each position has attributes deserving respect. In this chapter, we will consider the range of human attachments with both companion and production animals, the use of animals to serve a specific purpose, and the importance of animal-assisted therapy.

Many Species

The human-animal bond is often considered to be primarily a function of the relationship between people and their companion animals. As is keenly observed in *The New Work of Dogs,* intricate and often poorly understood relationships play out in our practices daily. This is true regardless of the species we treat.

Constant awareness of the life situations of our clients is needed to understand their bonds to their companion animals and their responses to our medical recommendations. For example, in my practice, a common situation is a client who must make a decision about euthanasia for a beloved pet—a pet that may represent the last tangible bond with their deceased partner. This resurrects precious memories of their lives together, with many clients reliving the loss of their loved one, a reminder of how difficult life is. Supporting the client before, during, and after the euthanasia is key to honoring the bond.

Production animals, laboratory animals, and zoo animals are often thought to be excluded from the notion of the human-animal bond. However, for each of those animals, there is a corresponding person who is legitimately concerned for the animal's safety and welfare. These animals are valued, and real concern is present for their well-being. This, too, is a form of the human-animal bond and must be respected. On family farms, an animal might be named and truly missed once having fulfilled its ultimate purpose.

Working Animals

Beyond pets and production animals, other types of bonded relationships include service animals, animals used in therapy settings, facility animals, and law enforcement/military animals.

Service animals are different from pets or therapy animals. True service animals provide specific tasks to assist as a "caregiver to their caregiver." The most common types of service animals are guide dogs, hearing assistance dogs, and dogs used for physical mobility assistance. More recently, service animal work has expanded to include additional species (eg, monkeys) and to provide alerts and assistance for people who have seizures, diabetes, or autism, as well as alerts and assurance for those with post-traumatic stress disorder. These animals are an integral part of their owner's lives, and the depth of their bond is extensive. Like other animals, service animals have a "worth" that is associated with financial considerations of medical or surgical treatment, plus the additional considerable investment in training. But there is also a psychosocial component for the owner. These animals are a true extension of the owner, by virtue of allowing their owners to live normal lives. As veterinarians, we must be aware that exceptional communication is needed to ensure the health and welfare of both parties when we make recommendations.

Many animals, particularly dogs, function as therapy animals. True therapy animals have special training and have been evaluated by specific organizations that attest to the animal's temperament and skills. Unfortunately, the quality of these evaluations is not always optimal. However, if well trained and with a skilled handler, these animals can have true therapeutic effect that extends well beyond that of animals used in animal-assisted activities. For example, dogs used in visitation programs ("pet therapy") are unlikely to be true therapy animals but still provide a great benefit to patients, visitors, and staff of facilities by alleviating stress, giving the patient some control, normalizing family communications, and providing both distraction and amusement.

Facility animals, which are generally dogs, are similar to true service animals. The difference is that their primary bond is with their handler, while they lend assistance and therapeutic intervention to others. These animals may be used to convince human patients that they can tolerate a procedure, to comfort them throughout an intensive examination, or to encourage them to complete a therapy or take their medication. They can also help staff to decompress during crises or after a particularly difficult or emotional loss of a patient. Like service animals, facility animals are associated with a high financial cost. They may be viewed by the facility owner as a financial investment to be protected (like a production animal), yet by their handler as a much loved and exceptionally skilled pet. These two differing viewpoints and types of bonds are sometimes at odds, and determining who is the true decision-maker can be a challenge.

Law enforcement and military animals are less likely than other working animals to be encountered in private practice. Working with these animals as a partner/protector/tool creates a strong bond, one likely different from what we might ever envision—bringing complexities that may require assistance from a professional in psychology, psychiatry, or social work. As is the case with facility animals, there is potential for a disconnect between the actual owner and the handler of the animals. These waters must be carefully approached, and ensuring clear communication with everyone involved is crucial to success.

What About Us?

Lastly, we cannot ignore the bond between veterinarians and their patients. This bond is real as well and, at times, may be in direct conflict to the bond (or lack thereof) between an animal and its owner. We must remain mindful of the mental and emotional toll this can take on us. We owe it to ourselves and our patients to be vigilant and to seek help when it is necessary.

You must be willing to do some soul searching and careful examination of your own biases and preconceptions to understand these permutations of the human-animal bond. As with many things in life, openness and careful consideration of all factors surrounding your patients is needed to fully honor the human-animal bond and the critical role it plays in our profession and our world.

Further Reading

- Burch MR, Bustad LK, Duncan SL, et al. The role of pets in therapeutic programmes. In: *The Waltham Book of Human-Animal Interaction: Benefits and Responsibilities of Pet Ownership.* Pergamon; 1995:55–69. Accessed Feb 1, 2020. https://habricentral.org/resources/4129

- Germone MM, Gabriels RL, Guérin NA, et al. Animal-assisted activity improves social behaviors in psychiatrically hospitalized youth with autism. *Autism.* 2019;23(7):1740–1751.

- Katz J. *The New Work of Dogs: Tending to Life, Love, and Family.* Villard (Random House); 2003.

ASSESSMENT, DIAGNOSIS, AND THERAPEUTIC PLAN

Dana G. Allen, DVM, MSc, DACVIM

"Observe, record, tabulate, communicate. Use your five senses. Learn to see, learn to hear, learn to feel, learn to smell, and know that by practice alone you can become expert."

–Sir William Osler

As a veterinarian, you will be challenged every day to solve puzzles. Through the skills you have developed during veterinary school, you will be able to decipher your patient's presenting signs, arrive at a diagnosis, and formulate an appropriate treatment.

The Appointment

The appointment is the first step in assessing your patient. Before you enter the exam room, take a look at the patient's record so you are familiar with the animal's signalment. Even before you set eyes on the patient, this will give you some building blocks to tackle the case. Age, sex, breed, and weight can all be significant clues. For example, if the animal is a neonate or young, you will want to be alert to congenital or hereditary conditions. Likewise, certain breeds are predisposed to specific conditions, which can be congenital or hereditary or develop later in life. Another reason to be sure you know the breed is that what may look like a mixed breed may in fact be a rare and expensive animal. Your credibility with the client is key to establishing a good veterinarian-client relationship.

120 — VETERINARIAN-CLIENT-PATIENT RELATIONSHIP

During the appointment, you will gather the history and conduct a physical examination, both powerful tools in determining a diagnostic plan. In medicine of any kind, emphasis is placed on collecting data and developing a minimum database. How useful is a complete history and physical examination? In a study completed at a human hospital in the United States, 56% of cases were correctly diagnosed by completing the history and 73% by completing the physical examination. I expect veterinary medicine is likely no different.

The Importance of Communication

Be sure to always greet your client and introduce yourself as Dr. _____ [insert surname], not as Dr. Bob or Dr. Jane. You have earned the right and respect that the title deserves. Likewise, you should also address your client professionally.

Clients usually want to start their side of the conversation by telling you the primary problem(s) for which the animal is being presented. Be courteous, listen, and hear the client out. Practice "active listening" by paraphrasing what your client has told you to be sure you understand each other. Good communication is a major factor in developing a relationship in which your client feels respected and valued, leading to increased client satisfaction, retention, and referrals. Good communication is also a major factor in decreasing liability.

History

In addition to the animal's signalment (age, sex, breed, weight), other basic information to gather includes the animal's appetite and diet (usual type of food and amount fed, including treats), water intake, and any clinical signs such as coughing, sneezing, vomiting, or any change in urine or feces. You'll also want to ask how long the problem has been going on. Other general questions may include whether the animal is indoors only or also spends time outdoors. You may want to ask if there is a travel history and, if so, where to and for how long? A question that is often overlooked is if there are other pets in the household and their state of health.

This basic history can guide you toward the right body system(s) to investigate further. More specific history is developed by asking questions pertinent to the primary issue and changes in any other body system. If the animal is exhibiting a particular behavior, asking the client to take a video of the behavior when the animal is in its usual environment can be extremely helpful.

When posing questions to clients, make the questions open-ended or neutral, rather than questions that elicit a simple "yes" or "no" or questions that lead clients to provide the answer they think you want to hear. For example, if you ask whether the animal is drinking a lot of water, the client may answer "yes," thinking that this is normal behavior. A better question is "How much water is your pet drinking?"

Physical Examination

Before beginning an examination, you should assess every patient for signs of aggression or fear biting by noting body posture and behavior. For example, does the pet cower in the corner of the examination room and growl? If there is any indication that an animal may be dangerous, take precautions appropriate for the species to protect yourself, staff members, and the owner. If the patient is bright, alert, and cooperative, you should still socialize yourself with the animal before abruptly starting a physical exam.

The most important principle of performing good physical examinations is to *develop a consistent, systematic approach—and to use it every time.* You will miss more by not looking than by not knowing! The physical examination has two phases. First, the observational examination includes assessment of alertness, responsiveness, general behavior, gait, body condition, and hair coat. Second is the hands-on examination, which usually begins at the head and moves toward the rear (ie, "from nose to toes to tail"), and includes thoracic auscultation and abdominal palpation.

Record evidence of your physical examination rather than inference. For example, document "dog has pale mucous membranes," rather than "dog is anemic." Be aware how expectations can affect your examination. You tend to find what it is you are looking for. Also remember that animals present with clinical signs, not symptoms. A symptom is a subjective observation made by a human patient, such as "It hurts here" or "I feel hot." In contrast, a clinical sign occurring in a patient (human or veterinary) is objective and can be seen or measured by others.

Keeping track of your patients' weight is worth a special note. It is estimated that more than 100 million dogs and cats in the United States are overweight or obese, up from 80 million only 5 years ago. Many owners are truly not aware of the healthy weight range for their pet, and you can advise them on an appropriate diet, feeding, and exercise plan. Monitoring weight loss or gain is important to assure improvement, or to identify lack of progress and the need for additional intervention.

Use All Your Senses

As you conduct the physical examination, use all your senses. Again, more is missed by not looking than by not knowing.

What do you see as the animal walks around the exam room? Is the animal lame? Is there a head tilt? Look at the condition of the haircoat and skin. Check the nose, eyes, and ears for a discharge or other abnormalities. Examine the color of the mucous membranes. Examine the skin for signs of pruritus (self-abrasions, discoloration of the fur from excessive licking) and external parasites. Do you see pustules, papules, or other cutaneous pathology? Carefully examine all four paws, including nails, nailbeds, and footpads. Be sure to check between the toes of all four feet for evidence of irritation, masses, or foreign bodies.

What does the animal smell like? Bad teeth and gums are a

common source of a bad odor. But an unusual or more subtle odor may be a significant clue. The mouth and breath of an animal with diabetes mellitus tends to smell "fruity," like the aroma of decomposing apples. Liver disease may impart a fishy odor to the breath. A yeast infection of the skin or ears may smell a little like cheese popcorn. An animal in kidney failure may smell like dried hops or malt due to the high concentration of ammonia in the urine. Animals with digestive issues may have foul-smelling gas.

Your hands and fingers can reveal a great deal of information about many body systems. Run your hands over the animal's entire body surface. This quick overview can detect cutaneous and subcutaneous masses. Assess the texture of the skin. Does it feel thicker or thinner than normal? Is it normal, greasy, or dry? Assess hydration, but keep in mind that skin "tenting" is an insensitive test and may be abnormally prolonged in animals that have lost a significant amount of body fat. The abdominal wall should be palpated to check for masses and for any hernias, including umbilical hernias, especially in pediatric patients. Palpate the various organs for size, shape, and consistency, and palpate all lymph nodes. Is any area of the body swollen or painful? Pressure can be placed over the vertebrae to detect neck and/or back pain. If you have observed any signs of lameness, try to localize the origin to a limb (and area on that limb) by palpation, flexion, and extension. Palpate the joints to detect any joint effusions, pain, or heat. Perform a rectal examination if there are signs of anal sac or rectal disease, or in intact male dogs to detect prostate issues.

What do you hear on the physical examination? Abnormal heart sounds may be associated with a murmur or an arrhythmia such as atrial fibrillation, heart block, or premature ventricular contractions. Listen especially carefully in pediatric patients for congenital heart disease and in senior patients for valvular conditions. Evaluate the respiratory system, beginning with breathing pattern, rate, and character, followed by auscultation for any abnormal sounds such as wheezes or rales/crackles. While you have your stethoscope handy, don't forget to listen for gut sounds.

The last sense is taste. Years ago, physicians would taste the urine of patients with suspected diabetes mellitus and, so, were known as "water tasters." If the urine tasted sweet, diabetes was diagnosed. In 1674, Dr. Thomas Willis described such urine as "wonderfully sweet as if it were imbued with honey or sugar." A year later, the word "mellitus" was added to the term diabetes, meaning honey. Thankfully, those days are gone by, and I am not suggesting that you put anything from a patient in your mouth. On the other hand, from the perspective of the patient, taste is an important sense. When an animal loses its sense of taste or smell, it may not want to eat. A host of diseases can affect taste and smell, but the first places to look are the mouth and nose.

More Communication

Clients often best remember the first thing you tell them, so if you are uncertain of the diagnosis, tell them so before discussing the possibilities and what you think is the most likely. Certain situations will call for you to communicate in a particularly thoughtful and/or sensitive way. If after you complete the history and physical examination, you suspect a serious condition (eg, lymphosarcoma), be honest with your client but emphasize the need for confirmation as something else may possibly be at play. Allow the client some time to digest devastating news, especially when a terminal diagnosis has been confirmed.

Communicating costs is also important. Before undertaking major diagnostic testing and evaluation, you should provide your client with an itemized estimate and update it as needed. As much as possible, the diagnostic plan should include next steps. If the client has overspent their budget on extensive testing, they may be understandably upset to find they are unable to afford treatment and follow-up care. If clients say, "Cost is of no concern," beware! They may be voicing love for their pet without taking account of their financial status. Having a policy of requiring a deposit of a certain percentage of estimated costs is prudent for both client and veterinarian.

Diagnostic Plan

The goal of the diagnostic plan is to verify initial problems, localize problem(s) to organ or body systems, identify potential pathologic findings, and rule in or rule out specific underlying causes. Clinical presentation of disease often varies because many clinical signs are nonspecific (eg, weakness, lethargy, anorexia), or it may be early in the disease course and definitive signs have not yet developed.

Consider if the patient's presentation conforms to a previously studied picture of disease. This is pattern recognition, but it is only the start of the diagnostic process. It's important to check the record (if available) to see if the patient has been treated for this malady before, and, if so, how and what was the response? From this point, list each problem, your assessment, and plans to address it. Take the time to be complete and systematic as you analyze the patient's history and your observations.

A routine set of diagnostic screening tests, generally a complete blood count, biochemical profile, urinalysis, and fecal exam, are typically performed to identify abnormalities and establish baseline values. Other diagnostic tests, such as radiography or other imaging, endoscopy, biopsy, culture and sensitivity, etc, are recommended as warranted by the presenting signs, or if abnormalities are identified in the initial tests. Aside from a diagnostic process, routine screening tests may also be performed as part of an annual health check, particularly for very young or old patients.

Testing can indicate the severity of illness, as well as help predict the clinical course and prognosis, the likely response to treatment, and the actual response to treatment. Remember that some test values can be out of the reference range and yet that individual is healthy. Test results must be interpreted in conjunction with the history, clinical signs, and the findings on the physical examination. Also remember that this interpretation may differ between clinicians and even with the same clinician at a different time. Medicine is an art.

Create a list of differential diagnoses in every case. Scoring schemes, algorithms, and decision trees can be useful problem-solving tools to organize clinical data and assess complex disorders. Making a checklist for diagnostic protocols can help ensure that you don't miss possibilities and that you avoid blind spots. The dulling of Occam's razor is a fundamental guiding principle in logic and science. Attributed to William of Ockham, an English Franciscan friar and scholarly philosopher, it states that the simplest hypothesis that explains a set of observations is usually the right one. In the diagnostic realm, this means that the temptation to have a simple answer to a complicated problem is powerful for patients and doctors alike. So, when is the time to look further? If a single cause can't explain all the data from the physical examination and laboratory testing, then it's time to look for a different or an additional cause.

Therapeutic Plan

A treatment plan is based on the history and results of the physical examination and diagnostic tests, with the goal of providing both specific and supportive therapy. Another part of every therapeutic plan is client education, which should include discussion of the patient's short- and long-term prognosis, as well as prognosis with or without therapy. If the patient has been hospitalized, specific discharge instructions should be provided to the client, including a demonstration of how to provide any at-home treatments (eg, administering eye or ear drops, cleaning wounds). Allow clients an opportunity to practice such treatments before leaving to ensure they will be able to provide the necessary at-home care. Follow-up is critical to monitor the animal's condition and response to treatment. Lack of follow-up is one of the biggest reasons for treatment failure.

Favorable outcomes associated with our treatments do not necessarily prove that our diagnoses or treatments were correct. If treatment is ineffective, then the diagnosis should be reviewed. Always keep a short list of alternatives for every situation, even when you think you have the answer. A good first step is to repeat the physical examination and any diagnostic tests to determine any change from the previous visit. More sophisticated or invasive diagnostic testing (eg, endoscopy, organ biopsy, surgical exploration), obtaining a second opinion, or consulting a specialist may also be indicated.

If you recommend referral to a specialist or the client requests it, immediately and gracefully transfer all needed information. This is the best way to support your patient and will reflect well upon you.

The Medical Record

After you graduate, you may find that the medical records you keep on your patients may become more abbreviated than when you were in school. Even so, you should continue to document the patient's history, results of the physical examination and any diagnostic testing, your assessment, treatment plans, and monitoring and recheck recommendations. It's also a good idea to keep a record of your discussions with the client. The medical record must be clear and complete so that any veterinarian reviewing it can understand the reason for the previous visit and what was done to address the problem(s).

Further Reading

- Bruyette D, ed. *Clinical Small Animal Internal Medicine.* Wiley Blackwell; 2020.

- Kelly JA. Acronyms on vet charts—what the heck do they mean. Accessed Jan 9, 2021. https://www.catster.com/lifestyle/cat-health-vet-records-charts

- National Academies of Sciences, Engineering, and Medicine. *Improving Diagnosis in Health Care.* The National Academies Press; 2015. https://doi.org/10.17226/21794

- Nelson RW, Couto CG, eds. *Small Animal Internal Medicine.* 6th ed. Elsevier; 2019.

- Sackett DL, Haynes RB, Tugwell P, et al. *Clinical Epidemiology: A Basic Science for Clinical Medicine.* 2nd ed. Little, Brown & Company; 1991.

- Sandler G. The importance of the history in the medical clinic and the cost of unnecessary tests. *Am Heart J.* 1980;100:928–931.

- Tilley LP, Smith FWK Jr, Sleeper MM, Brainard BM, eds. Blackwell's *Five-Minute Veterinary Consult: Canine and Feline.* 7th ed. Wiley Blackwell; 2021.

- Woolever DR. The art and science of clinical decision making. Accessed Jan 9, 2021. https://www.aafp.org/fpm/2008/0500/fpm20080500p31.pdf

CLIENT COUNSELING, COMFORT CARE, AND EUTHANASIA

Kathleen Cooney, DVM, CHPV, CCFP

"Don't count the days, make the days count."

–Mohammed Ali

Early in my veterinary career, it became clear that my role with clients was going to be equal parts counselor and medical director. Clients often invite us deep into their story to support them while they care for their pets, especially as the pet approaches the end of its life. And we need to be worthy of their trust in us. What it takes to both love and provide for a pet can at times feel monumental.

Over the years, I have found client support to be my favorite part of being a veterinarian. As I honed my communication skills, as you will too, my appreciation for the depth of comfort veterinarians can provide is profound. Every appointment is an opportunity to strengthen trust, to practice with authenticity and integrity, and to elevate a client's perception of our profession. Veterinarians are held in high regard by the pet-loving community not only for our ability to heal and protect, but also for our capacity to love and guide all who seek our help.

Communicating Well

Good communication will be at the heart of your work. To support the dying, we rely on empathy and understanding. Gone are the days of paternal communication, in which a client is only told what to do and how to do it. We practice in a time when a sincere exchange of thoughts and opinions on both sides establishes better delivery of care. It doesn't matter what's behind the conversation to recognize how beneficial it is to speak openly and honestly with one another. As practitioners, we must focus on learning the full story, gaining an appreciation of inherent challenges to our recommendations, and modifying any and all treatments to align with what's truly possible. Patient care is a marriage of good communication, counseling, and medical acumen.

When it comes to difficult, emotional conversations around the end of a patient's life, you will be called to assist clients in perhaps their darkest hour. This huge responsibility can be filled with uncertainty. The important thing during these interactions is to slow down, take some deep breaths, and let your natural abilities rise to the surface. Follow the golden rule of treating others the way you want to be treated. Think about what you would need if you were the client and the dying pet was yours. Although we want to do all we can to support the bereaved, it is beyond our capability to fix the pain and sadness. Dr. Alan Wolfelt, noted bereavement expert, recommends this simple approach: *"Mouth closed, ears open, and presence available."* It is one of the best means of consoling clients.

Hospice and Comfort Care

My professional work is dedicated to hospice, palliative care, and gentle euthanasia, and I would like to share some insights learned over the years. Many have mentored me, including human physicians, through the written word and conversation, all to help hone the skills needed to protect and cherish the end-of-life experience. A dying patient requires special care, both emotionally and physically. Animal hospice is all about increasing comfort while decreasing signs. To palliate means to cloak or hide the disease(s) and allow the patient to live as normally as possible until such time when the maladies become too great. There can be palliative medicine without hospice, but there can be no hospice without palliative medicine. You will be asked to practice with great proficiency as you aid in a pet's end-of-life journey. A solid understanding of how the body works, and dies, will ensure you are prepared to meet the demands of the dying. Continue to learn as much as you can. It will open up options for you, both medically and spiritually.

Comfort care is provided to both client and pet. They are bonded, which means both will participate in the end-of-life experience. The client will be the one applying daily medical therapies and feeling the emotional weight of the loss. Clients need you to help them understand what the disease may bring, how to recognize signs of pain, and ways to provide comfort to their pet at all hours. Clients are often very afraid. Education and consistent communication make the difference between a scary journey and a safe one. Knowledge is power and can lessen fear-based decision-making. Pets will require both physical and emotional support so as to live with dignity, joy, and comfort until the time of death. You will aid pets by closely balancing therapies they can tolerate against what brings them daily fulfillment. We must explore their will to live against what we know is coming, all while honoring the client's wishes. By giving clients choices, you return to them a sense of balance in a time when they feel lost.

Because a dying patient's medical needs are great, experts advocate for a team approach. This is one way that veterinary medicine can emulate human medicine. Since the onset of human hospice, physicians, nurses, counselors, chaplains, and others have worked synergistically to manage care. In my hospice service, I have a long list of trusted professionals ready to support my clients and patients. We have banded together to share our collective talents with one mission in mind: to prevent suffering and protect the human-animal bond. And we must remember that everyone intimately connected to the dying pet can be on the team, including extended family members, friends, groomers, dog walkers, pet sitters, etc. This will help lessen the burden of care for the immediate family members.

The Art of Gentle Euthanasia

A veterinarian's role is to use whatever means necessary to relieve animal suffering, and this includes the delicate task of euthanasia. Often looked at as a failure when cure or palliation is unobtainable, I see it differently. What a kind gesture we can make to ensure no further struggle remains. Dr. Frank McMillan, veterinarian and philosopher, noted the following in a 2001 *JAVMA* article: *"When it comes to the sick and injured, euthanasia is not an act to end a life. This is not its purpose, and not the outcome we are striving to achieve. Euthanasia is an act to end discomfort. Death is the unfortunate, unavoidable, and unintentional effect of achieving this goal."* I find this sentiment very profound and have shared it numerous times with my clients to reassure them. It is agonizing for a client to choose to end the life of a beloved friend. Our task is to lessen this burden by delivering the most gentle and peaceful death possible.

An artful delivery of euthanasia services goes much smoother when you've readied your emotional and physical self. Here are the fundamental steps I have learned to ease my clients' hearts while strengthening my euthanasia work:

1. Relax your mind and body through deep, slow breathing. Let all tension go.
2. Focus on the power of the human-animal bond.
3. Build rapport with the client and your patient.
4. Take time to listen to your client's stories. Embrace your communication skills.
5. Deliver a technically strong euthanasia.

There will come a time when your client feels the time is right for euthanasia, but you do not. Other times, you will advocate for it, and your client will resist. Have patience. Seek to find common ground and educate clients on all possible outcomes. Regardless of said outcome, focus your energy on the dutiful steps you took to support your clients and patients, not the outcome itself. This is paramount if we are to live in a state of "compassion satisfaction" rather than "compassion fatigue." Ending the life of an animal is laden with complexities. Go easy on yourself. Know your limits and stick to them. Stay true to who you are.

You may find end-of-life work speaks to you. Up until the mid 2010s, it was almost unheard of that a newly minted veterinarian would devote his or her career to animal hospice or euthanasia-centric work. How fortunate are we to have such resources available that allow for this kind of specialty. If you find that partnering with clients and patients during a time of transition appeals to you, explore it. One of the most gratifying things about veterinary medicine is all the opportunities that await you. Upon graduating from veterinary school, I envisioned myself in traditional general practice. What I found was a calling to support grieving and bereaved clients while providing the smoothest death I could for my patients, either naturally or through the gift of euthanasia.

Every one of our patients will have an end-of-life journey, be it brief or extended. Therefore, all of us will need to be stewards of death at some point. It is an honor to help a family say goodbye to a beloved companion. It is the last chapter in hopefully a long and meaningful life. Remember that what your clients, patients, and colleagues expect of you is to be kind, to use your knowledge, and to guide with compassion. Whenever in doubt, ask yourself "What's the most loving thing I can do right now?"

Further Reading

- McMillan F. Rethinking euthanasia: death as an unintentional outcome. *J Amer Vet Med Assoc.* 2001;219(9):1204–1206.

- Wolfelt A. *When Your Pet Dies: A Guide to Mourning, Remembering and Healing.* Companion Press; 2004.

- Companion Animal Euthanasia Training Academy. Utilizing euthanasia to reduce compassion fatigue. Accessed Jan 10, 2021. https://caetainternational.com/utilizing-euthanasia-to-reduce-compassion-fatigue/

A BALANCED LIFE

BALANCE AND REFLECTION

Susan P. Cohen, DSW

"Be aware of wonder. Live a balanced life - learn some and think some and draw and paint and sing and dance and play and work every day some."

–Robert Fulghum

Do you save interesting messages from fortune cookies? They say things like, "Never throw caution to the wind" and "A good memory is fine, but the ability to forget is the one true test of greatness." My all-time favorite is "There's more to balance than not falling over." Balance is living with joy, sometimes. Balance is being bored, sometimes. Balance is the family you want, and a job you like, and healthy physical activity, and spiritual connections, and an art course or collecting old bottles or playing the trumpet. You can have it all but not at the same time.

The trick to finding balance is to pay attention to your life, to reflect. Ask yourself questions. How do people work hard in a satisfying career without losing themselves in it? How do people with drive and commitment at work still have a personal life? How do people continue to love their career, year after year, even when it's hard? How does anyone realize it's time to change, because the "same-old" doesn't fit any more? And how can a dedicated professional live a life without regret?

Like many other professionals, veterinarians often have trouble with what is referred to as "work-life balance." For some, this seems like a bad joke, a condition they will never encounter, and a sad state of affairs. With attention to what we are good at, what needs doing, and what gives us joy, we can live a life with both job satisfaction and good relationships, creativity, and personal growth. The answer to finding balance is to reflect on your day, year, health, happiness.

Causes of Career Stress

Veterinary medicine has always been a stressful profession, but the causes have changed. In the early 1980s, the medical knowledge base exploded, making it hard to keep up. Veterinary schools didn't teach client communication or self-care. Stress was a badge of honor. Strong client emotion was avoided. A common myth was that if owners were allowed to witness their pet's euthanasia, they would faint, hit their head, and sue the veterinarian. Veterinarians were instructed to say, "Fluffy is suffering and should be put down now. Go ahead and leave; you want to remember her as she was when she was well."

Veterinary education was slow to recognize that clients might be willing to go farther and spend more on a pet than previously thought. The dean of one school explained why, despite requests, a social worker wasn't needed on staff. "There would only be one-two people a year who would need one, and those would be dog lovers. When I was in practice, I never recommended a feline treatment that cost more than $25, because who would spend more than $25 on a cat?"

These days, stress in veterinary medicine comes from different sources. Clients expect more than ever. They no longer blindly take the word of professionals. They "Google," they read, and they ask questions. A lot of questions. And when frustrated or dissatisfied clients don't like the answers, they often challenge the veterinarian and seek advice elsewhere.

Stress from money issues has escalated. Because diagnostic and treatment options have become more numerous and sophisticated, veterinary bills have skyrocketed. Clients are often under pressure to make life-and-death decisions for a beloved family member based on economics. As a result, clients may pressure their veterinarian to lower fees or cut corners medically. In the worst cases, clients may threaten to ruin the veterinarian's reputation on social media.

Stress from financial issues also stems from heavy student debt carried by many young veterinarians and the growing corporatization of veterinary practice. Associates' incomes, and therefore their ability to pay off debt, can depend on how much clients are billed, adding to pressure to maximize practice revenue. Veterinary medicine starts to feel that it's less about saving animals and more about generating revenue.

The rise of large organizations, vaccine clinics, and specialty groups has forced all practices to adapt, sometimes in unhealthy ways. Less healthy businesses extend hours for no extra pay, encourage veterinarians to perform procedures that generate high revenue, and retain clients that are rude to employees. Managers overbook, leaving no time for a real lunch. Staff members are ordered to see any client who comes in before the door is locked. Leaving on time is frowned on. Martyrdom is celebrated.

The Real World

Potential veterinarians used to begin their careers by shadowing a practitioner or working with local farmers in the summers. This behind-the-scenes veterinary experience, followed by the rigorous training in veterinary school that included hands-on work in everyday cases and procedures, allowed new graduates to enter general practice confident they were ready for almost anything. These days, veterinary students enter school with less time spent in a practice. Because the number of specialists and schools has increased, some students say they have to compete for cases with interns and residents. They graduate feeling very good at making referrals to experts but less sure of their own skills.

Most veterinarians have a passion for animals, along with science and service. That desire does not always come with an extroverted personality, an ease with coworker and client emotions, and an acceptance of personal imperfections. In fact, perfectionism is almost a hallmark of medical professionals. Perfectionism is not striving to do your best; it is beating up yourself and everyone else over anything and everything that could have gone better. Perfectionists trap themselves in the belief that everything rests on their shoulders. If they don't "do it all," disaster may follow.

Many new graduates enter practice with excitement and hope but little thought about the type of environment they need to thrive. Do you like a formal atmosphere where employees use titles and don't socialize after work? Or a casual and friendly environment, with weekly pizza staff meetings? When a practice says, "We offer mentoring," does that mean discussions on the spot? Daily rounds? "Come find me if you really need to"? "A week of learning the paperwork and then you're on your own, because I'm headed out for a month's vacation"?

The evidence that the pressure of practice is taking a toll comes in anecdotal accounts and social research. Practice owners lament the difficulty of finding associates, technicians, and other employees. In one small survey from 2016, the most common answer to "Would you become a veterinarian again?" was "no." Even more alarming, several studies have found that the number of veterinarians and technicians with suicidal ideation is significantly higher than that in the general population.

Finding Balance

While practice and people issues certainly cause stress, veterinarians also need to reflect and look inside themselves. Career satisfaction depends on much more than accumulated knowledge and hard work. So, what can you do to have a satisfying career in veterinary medicine, an enjoyable private life, and an appreciation for yourself? You check in with yourself at regular intervals—a little every day, a lot once a year.

For example, take a minute at the end of every day to ask yourself a few questions:

- What did I accomplish?
- What did I learn?
- What went well and what didn't?
- What do I have to be grateful for today? Some days you will be grateful that your day wasn't worse. That's okay. It still counts.

Have a more serious check-in once a year. Pick a day—New Year's Day, your birthday, the first day of school—to ask yourself the big questions:

- Am I happy with my life 75% of the time?
- Does my job make me feel useful?
- How would I like to develop professionally?
- Who are my friends, the ones I can turn to if I break a leg or need a lawyer or just need someone to listen? If I don't have enough social support, how can I develop more friendships?
- If someone asked about my hobbies, how would I answer?
- How much time with others and how much time alone do I want? Is that how much I have?
- Is my life in balance?

If you don't like the answers to these questions, what can you change?

It's a three-step process. First, ask yourself what you do well. Ironically, many accomplished people have a hard time with this question, because when things come easily, they don't recognize their own abilities and talents. If that's the case, ask your friends how they see you. When do your coworkers call on you?

Second, what needs doing? Has anything in the practice environment changed or not changed that you can address?

Perhaps you could suggest a change in the technology being used that could save money or time. Or maybe you'd like to explore adding a new service that could add to the bottom line. When you find your niche, even a small one, you may find yourself reinvigorated.

Third, think about what makes you happy. At work, what are the tasks you like best? Try to do more of them. Outside of work, what excites you? What makes you feel your best? Schedule time for those activities to make sure they happen. Do you want more time with your family? More time to play guitar? Time to train for your first marathon? Cultivating an artistic talent or other hobby can bring you joy and renew your spirit, helping to compensate for occasional exhaustion and disappointment at your job. This is balance.

Your Health

Protecting your mental and physical health is another part of balance. Veterinarians have big hearts and want to help as many animals as possible. Many have trouble saying "no" and setting limits. A client calls or shows up at the last minute. Your boss asks you to take on additional workload without additional compensation. You need to attend an online continuing education class, but your kids are squabbling in the next room. Your headaches are getting worse, but your work schedule doesn't mesh with getting an appointment with your physician. Remember that if you don't take care of yourself, you cannot help anyone else, at least not for long.

Begin to take note of the times you feel pressured to do things against your better judgment. You might even write down the time, place, and circumstances to see whether you uncover a pattern. Write down your feelings, too. Unexpressed emotions can drive you out of a field you used to love when self-awareness and a little gumption could give you a long and happy career.

Learning to assert your needs and set boundaries takes practice. Start small, in ways that carry less risk. For example, if you find too much conversation wearing or that you get snarky when you haven't eaten all day, try announcing that you'll be taking a half-hour lunch break in your car. Request a meeting with the staff or your manager to make this happen. Taking short "power naps" (15–20 minutes) can be invigorating and recharge your batteries for the rest of the day. Read articles on negotiating. Watch other people who seem to get their needs met and adopt any of their techniques that you feel comfortable using. Then, when you feel ready, take a deep breath and say what you really want. The other person may not enjoy the experience or praise you for it, but at least you will have reclaimed your authentic self.

Finding your balance through reflection applies to more significant concerns as well. Few of us live a life of perfect behavior. We reach for a chocolate doughnut instead of celery sticks. We turn on the TV after dinner instead of taking a brisk walk. We splurge on another gadget instead of adding to our savings account. If, however, you observe that you frequently do things that you know are not good for you—overeating junk food, drinking excessive alcohol, spending recklessly—these are signs that your stress or predispositions are leading you in the wrong direction. You might even find yourself feeling hopeless or thinking dark thoughts.

If any of these behaviors sound familiar, seek the help of a counselor or therapist. Needing support is not a weakness. Some veterinarians think they need to hide their problems to protect their license and liability insurance. Or they live in small communities with few choices of therapy professionals. Plus, people who are depressed or caught in an addiction may find it hard to marshal the energy to reach out. You must overcome these concerns. Start with your physician, clergyperson, or someone else you trust. Check websites and directories for places that have therapists on staff, such as mental health clinics or graduate programs. If you have more than one option, arrange an introductory session with each professional to see whether you form a good connection. Tell the therapist what you want to work on and feel free to say how you think the process is going. A good mental health clinician will collaborate with you to create an environment where you can heal and grow.

Your Life

The way to reach the end of your career satisfied with your accomplishments, your relationships, your health, and your pleasures is to give your life some thought as you go through it. Be the scientist of your own experience. Take a moment every day to observe events and your feelings about them. Learn from them. Remember that you are entitled to be happy. Things will go wrong. You will make mistakes. You will have bad moods and so will others. Pay attention to things that get in your way and get support to change them. Pay even more attention to what makes you feel healthy and content, the things that give you joy. Life won't always be perfect, but remember, "There's more to balance than not falling over."

Further Reading

- Fisher R, Ury W. *Getting to Yes: Negotiating Agreement Without Giving In.* Penguin Books; 2011.

- Net RJ, Witte T, Spitzer EG, et al. Suicide risk for veterinarians and veterinary technicians. NIOSH Science Blog, CDC Centers for Disease Control and Prevention, 2019. Accessed Jan 10, 2021. https://blogs.cdc.gov/niosh-science-blog/2019/09/04/veterinary-suicide/

- Wise C. Vet school, would you do it again? Thoughts on why so many people are saying no! VetPrep, 2016. Accessed Jan 10, 2021. https://blog.vetprep.com/vet-school-would-you-do-it-again-why-so-many-are-saying-no

SELF-CARE

Marie Holowaychuk, DVM, DACVECC, CYT

"Self-care is giving the world the best of you,
instead of what's left of you."

–Katie Reed

The veterinary profession has changed dramatically in the last 50 years. Solo practitioners, individual coverage of "on-call," and the pressures of owning and running a business have been largely replaced by practices with multiple associate veterinarians, 24/7 emergency and referral centers, and practice management by designated individuals or corporations. There has also been a shift in focus from "living to work as a veterinarian" to "working as a veterinarian to live" as an individual with a flourishing personal life that includes time spent with family or friends and engagement in non-veterinary activities.

Yet, the incidence of mental illness and suicide among adults has increased, with a notably higher risk of suicide in veterinarians than in the general population. Commonly cited stressors in veterinary practice causing burnout, substance use, or compassion fatigue include growing financial concerns, client-related demands, and interpersonal conflict.

Substance Use Disorders

Substance use–related disorders can result in an inability to function effectively or perform necessary duties at work or home. The four C's describe the signs of a substance addiction:

Compulsion: the urge to use is intense and overwhelming.

Craving: the urge to use feels vital for survival, mimicking a physical need.

Consequences: use continues despite physical, mental, social, legal, or financial ramifications.

Control: the ability to control the amount or frequency of use is lost.

Substance addiction is a complex disorder and typically requires intervention and support from licensed professionals. If you notice any signs in yourself or a colleague, please reach out for help.

Compassion Fatigue

Compassion fatigue can impact veterinarians at different stages in their careers and is characterized by a physical and emotional exhaustion that occurs when a person is unable to rejuvenate with self-care and time away from work or intense work situations. Veterinarians can also experience compassion fatigue due to repeated situations of moral stress that are not acknowledged or are insufficiently addressed. Compassion fatigue accumulates over time and can affect veterinarians outside of work, unlike signs of burnout that are usually not readily apparent once someone is away from work. Behaviors such as detachment or avoidance, reduced sense of purpose in work, apathy, and isolation can be indicative of compassion fatigue.

Well-Being and Self-Care

Veterinarians, like caregivers in other professions, must balance care for others with care for themselves. In doing so, they will be better able to sustain themselves in the veterinary profession long-term and cultivate a life of mental and physical health and well-being.

Well-being promotes mental health and wellness and preserves an ability to thrive and maintain longevity in the veterinary profession. Studies show that US veterinarians have higher levels of well-being when they have higher income, minimal student debt, fewer hours (and not working evenings), and own their practice. High levels of well-being are also strongly associated with participating in healthy activities not related to work (eg, reading for pleasure, having a hobby), traveling, spending time with family, socializing with friends, exercising regularly, and being married or in a stable relationship.

Strategies and tools for preserving mental health and well-being are becoming more readily available to veterinarians; these include access to employee assistance programs with mental health support, provision of personal wellness days in addition to sick and vacation days, and online programs and tools promoting personal and professional well-being from veterinary medical associations. Many veterinary practices and conglomerates are changing the culture of veterinary medicine to foster mental health, work-life harmony, and well-being within and outside of the veterinary workplace.

Regardless, the responsibility for self-care ultimately rests on the individual. This cannot be overemphasized, given that we spend our workdays caring for patients, clients, and colleagues and other team members. As such, veterinarians have a moral and ethical obligation to prioritize self-care to ensure their well-being and to continue to care for patients and others while avoiding harm. Like the recommendation from flight attendants for passengers to first don their own oxygen mask before assisting another, veterinarians must first tend to their own needs or they will not be able to care for others.

Self-care is a self-initiated behavior that promotes good health and general well-being. Self-care involves a long-term plan to build up reserves to enhance resilience and manage stress. A not uncommon misconception is that self-care is easy, fun, enjoyable, and random, like ordering a tasty latte or taking a bubble bath.

However, the reality is that self-care can be tedious, challenging, and uncomfortable, and it almost always requires planning. Examples include getting recommended immunizations, scheduling an appointment with a counselor, spending time in nature, regularly setting aside your cell phone for a period of time, seeing a friend for coffee, learning a new language, setting boundaries at work, sorting out personal finances, and decluttering the home.

Coping strategies are not synonymous with self-care. Examples include binge-watching favorite television shows, having a drink after work, and ordering take-out after a long shift. Coping strategies are short-term means of dealing with difficulties or stress and—although they can be useful during a crisis when a person feels too tired or overwhelmed to plan anything else—they do not promote health. In fact, over time, they can be draining and result in a vicious cycle of not planning or prioritizing adequate self-care. In this situation, when times are stressful or the crisis mode persists, the option to support well-being may no longer be feasible.

The Eight Dimensions of Wellness

To ensure that their self-care practice is consistent and beneficial, veterinarians must take a proactive and holistic approach. Self-care strategies to promote health and well-being all foster one of the eight dimensions of wellness: physical, emotional, spiritual, social, intellectual, occupational, financial, and environmental. Each dimension interacts with the others to result in physical and mental health and wellness.

- *Physical wellness* is avoiding illness and maintaining a thriving lifestyle. This dimension includes adopting healthy habits such as routine medical exams, immunizations, safety precautions, appropriate sleep hygiene, a balanced diet, regular exercise, and care for minor illnesses. It also includes avoiding or minimizing behaviors such as excessive tobacco, drug, or alcohol use.

- *Emotional wellness* encompasses optimism, self-esteem, self-acceptance, and the ability to cope with feelings independently and with others. Strategies that foster wellness in this dimension include cultivating inner resources, building resilience, coping effectively with stressors, setting boundaries to manage expectations and time, having the capacity to notice and manage feelings, accepting limitations, and asking for help.

- *Spiritual wellness* involves seeking and having a meaning and purpose in life, as well as participating in activities that are consistent with your beliefs and values. It includes a deep appreciation for the complexity of life and the natural forces in the universe. Self-care strategies in this dimension include practicing gratitude, attending church services, listening to inspirational speakers, spending time in nature, or journaling as a form of reflection.

- *Social wellness* focuses on contributions to the community and personal relationships that, in turn, cultivate a sense of belonging. This dimension encourages taking an active role in communities or organizations, connecting with others, establishing supportive social networks, developing meaningful relationships, and creating safe and inclusive spaces.

- *Intellectual wellness* necessitates participating in mentally stimulating and creative activities in and outside of the veterinary profession. It fosters the ability to think critically, reason objectively, and explore new ideas and different points of view. Self-care strategies in this dimension emphasize lifelong learning and curiosity in the form of expanding knowledge, learning new skills, teaching others, and keeping up on current issues.

- *Occupational wellness* involves participating in work that provides personal satisfaction and life enrichment and aligns with individual values, goals, and lifestyle. This dimension requires taking a thoughtful and proactive approach to assessing personal satisfaction at work and using unique gifts, skills, and talents. Maintaining boundaries to ensure work-life separation is an essential self-care practice within this dimension.

- *Financial wellness* includes managing resources to live within one's means, making informed financial decisions and investments, setting realistic financial goals, and learning to prepare for short- and long-term needs, as well as emergencies. Self-care strategies in this dimension consist of managing debt, planning bill payments, and meeting regularly with financial advisors.

- *Environmental wellness* means engaging in a lifestyle that is respectful of one's surroundings. It requires understanding the dynamic relationship between the environment and the people within it, as well as understanding that environments have a tremendous impact on mental and physical well-being. Self-care strategies in this dimension include prioritizing safety, minimizing waste, decluttering, and recycling or reusing items whenever possible.

Setting Self-Care Goals

To assess your current situation and create a self-care plan, you must first review your current self-care practices and identify the wellness dimensions you wish to target. You can then set goals using the SMART acronym: specific, measurable, achievable, relevant, and timely. Then, identify the resources you will need to overcome any untoward resistance and achieve your goals.

For example, rather than stating a desire to improve physical wellness, instead plan to exercise for 30 minutes each day. This goal could be made even more specific and measurable by adding a particular activity to your calendar and reassessing in 1–3 months to determine its benefit. Other examples of SMART goals in the different wellness dimensions include the following:

- *Physical:* Increase sleep from 6 to 7 hours per day by setting a bedtime alarm and turning off screens 30 minutes before bedtime.
- *Emotional:* Schedule an appointment with a mental health professional before the end of the month by using an employee assistance program.
- *Spiritual:* Meditate for 10 minutes each morning after waking (using an application).
- *Social:* Block off time in the calendar for a weekly coffee outing with a close friend.
- *Intellectual:* Sign up for a class or online course to learn a new skill or language before the end of the quarter.
- *Occupational:* Establish boundaries with clients by setting expectations once or twice a year regarding availability in the form of an automated email, voicemail message, or practice policy.
- *Financial:* Meet with a financial planner annually to review debt load, current budget, and emergency funds and to plan for retirement.
- *Environmental wellness:* Spend 15 minutes each day to declutter the home living space or choose a closet or room to declutter every month. A daily walk in the park or nearby woods can also serve to declutter your mind.

Individuals respond to accountability in different ways, but most of us are better able to achieve our self-care goals when held externally accountable. This can be in the form of accountability partners, deadlines, scheduling, or other forms of oversight. When people are held externally accountable, they face consequences for not meeting their goals (eg, letting a workout buddy down, missing a deadline). Accountability can also be as simple as sharing a self-care goal or plan publicly (eg, social media, sticky note) to set an expectation so that others can check in to see how things are going. In family situations, a spouse or partner is very important in assisting with self-care and should be included in planning and supporting self-care goals.

Following up is vital to determine whether self-care goals have been met or additional resources or support are needed. Alternatively, unsuccessful self-care goals can be replaced by other goals. In the above example of an exercise goal, if a lack of time prevented success, possible options are waking up earlier, exercising over lunch, or using free online exercise classes for working out at home.

Put deadlines in your phone, write reminders in your calendar, and review your self-care plan every 3–6 months. Self-care plans evolve over time and must be revisited regularly and adjusted accordingly. When your self-care plans are successful and goals are met, acknowledging your good work is important. Likewise, be compassionate and forgive yourself if the goals are not met or sustainable. You can make new goals and put strategies in place for success the next time.

Further Reading

- American Veterinary Medical Association. Wellbeing. Accessed Jan 10, 2021. https://www.avma.org/resources-tools/well-being

- Dr. Marie Holowaychuk – Reviving Veterinary Medicine. Accessed Jan 10, 2021. https://marieholowaychuk.com/

- I Matter – Your Guide to a Happy Life as a Veterinarian. Accessed Jan 10, 2021. https://i-matter.ca/

- Mighty Vet. Accessed Jan 10, 2021. http://mightyvet.org

- Mind Matters Initiative. Accessed Jan 10, 2021. https://www.vetmindmatters.org/

MENTORS AND MENTORING

Craig N. Carter, DVM, MS, PhD, DACVPM, DSNAP

*"A mentor is someone who allows you to see
the hope inside yourself."*

–Oprah Winfrey

The term "mentor" comes from a character in Homer's classic poem *The Odyssey*. Mentor was a loyal friend of Odysseus. When Odysseus left for the Trojan War, he put Mentor in charge of his son Telemachus. Mentor built a relationship with Telemachus, while teaching, coaching, and counseling him. The term "mentor," as adopted in the English language, means an experienced and trusted advisor, someone who provides insight and shares knowledge with a less practiced associate. What qualities should a mentor have? Although certainly not an exhaustive list, good mentors should freely share their time, have a positive attitude, take a keen personal interest in their mentees, be enthusiastic about their future, be reachable and responsive, and be an expert in the field that their mentees are pursuing.

Early Mentors and the Early Influence of Osler

I have personally benefited immensely by those who graciously mentored me, and I have tried my level best to serve as a mentor for others as often as possible. My two most wonderful mentors have been my mother and my wife. My mother sent me James Herriot's *All Creatures Great and Small* for my birthday in 1973, a book that helped confirm my interest in veterinary medicine as a career. I owe much gratitude to my wife, who has encouraged me and supported my veterinary career pursuits for more than 30 years. The consistent and steadfast influence of these two amazing women has never left my side.

In the professional realm, one of my most cherished mentors, Dr. William McCulloch, taught infectious diseases, epidemiology, and veterinary public health during my time as a veterinary and graduate student at Texas A&M. One evening in 1986, he surprised me with a gift of his two-volume set by Cushing, *The Life of Sir William Osler*. Bill referenced Osler often in his lectures and enlightened me that Osler was known as the founder of modern medicine and veterinary pathology. The Spanish Flu pandemic, from January 1918 to December 1920, resulted in the deaths of an estimated 50 million people worldwide. Osler died of pneumonia and empyema caused by *Haemophilus influenzae* at age 70, on December 29, 1919, right in the middle of that pandemic outbreak. Cushing included these comments regarding the debilitated Osler, circa June or July 1918:

> The influenza epidemic at the time was just beginning and knowing Osler's condition and his susceptibility to pulmonary infections, his friends were greatly concerned about him. "W.O. grows thinner all the time and I can't have him lose another ounce of flesh, his bones will come through," was Lady Osler's comment at this time.

Another excellent book worthy of mention is *Osler: Inspirations from a Great Physician* by Charles S. Bryan. This book could also be entitled "Life 101," because as it contains eight chapters on how to discover your life's passion, connect with outstanding mentors, reach your goals, and have balance in your life. In Chapter 3, *Find Mentors: The Young Person's Friend,* Bryan speaks of what he calls the "four stages of the mentor-protégé relationship," which approximate the eight stages of mentorship that I outline below.

Bryan explains that Osler set out as an apprentice, later becoming an individual contributor, then rising to an increasingly effective mentor, and ultimately evolving into an organization influencer.

Mentors Throughout Life

Our need for mentorship is lifelong because we never stop learning. I firmly believe that mentoring is particularly significant for the pursuit of a multifaceted career such as veterinary medicine. In fact, I am doubtful that any person moving down this challenging path could be successful without a healthy dose of first-class mentorship along the way.

All of you pursuing (or recently having received) a veterinary degree will recall the first four steps of the eight-stage process below. Every stage benefits from proper mentorship.

1. Showing an early interest in animals, animal health, and a possible career in veterinary medicine (birth through high school)

2. Gaining relevant experiences with animals in a veterinary practice or on a farm (high school and during undergraduate education).

3. Choosing and enrolling in a pre-veterinary preparation program (high school, college level and possibly beyond)

4. Applying to veterinary school (college level and possibly beyond)

5. Completing a curriculum in veterinary medicine, deciding on a practice focus, and/or considering specialization (during veterinary training and beyond)

6. Graduating veterinary school and finding and starting your first job as a veterinarian

7. Gaining and maintaining competency as a practicing veterinarian (throughout all practice years)

8. Deciding about possibly leaving practice and training for an

alternative career in another area that requires or benefits from veterinary training

In stages 1–4, mentors include parents, other family members, possibly farm workers, high school teachers and counselors, college faculty members and advisors, and certainly the practicing veterinarians that a student has shadowed with or worked for along the way.

In stage 5, you have been accepted into a veterinary college and are faced with a rigorous 4-year curriculum. Seeking out one or more mentors can significantly help you transition into the first-year course of study (and beyond). Many students find the sheer number of semester course hours, homework, special projects, and other activities to be overwhelming. Mentors may be able to help you improve your organizational and task management skills, or perhaps suggest additional one-on-one study assistance if necessary. Joining student study groups is a handy peer mentoring option, ie, "learn from each other." When you enter your fourth year, mentors can help you select the optional clinical blocks/ rotations that best fit your goals and species focus. As you end your fourth year, mentors can coach you on how to develop and structure your resume, how best to apply for a job, what to expect in an interview process, and how to evaluate and decide about position job itself.

Stages 6 and 7 are the culmination of your hard work and the support of your family, professors, and mentors along the way— congratulations! No matter where you begin your career—private practice, academia, military, government, or industry—continue to seek out mentors to help you make a successful transition to your new job, to maintain competency, and to build your clinical skills through continuing education. Immediately consider joining national organizations such as the AVMA, regional and state veterinary associations, and local community and civic groups.

After completing your first year or two on the job, consider serving and taking leadership roles on relevant committees that you are passionate about (eg, an area of clinical medicine or surgery, shelter medicine, telemedicine). Be willing to contribute your time, knowledge, and experience to improve and advance veterinary medicine in your chosen discipline. Your contributions will help to improve your practice and better serve your clients and the health of their animals. Once stabilized in your career as a veterinarian, be watchful for younger colleagues who need a coach or a mentor. By "passing the torch," you can now advise others who are following the path you took just a few years before.

You may reach stage 8 at some point, depending on the level of your career satisfaction, evolving goals, and other life circumstances. It is crucial to maintain an open mind throughout your career. Some clinicians begin to experience burnout after several years in practice or become curious about an alternative career. One of the truly wonderful things about this profession is that there are myriad ways to use your veterinary degree and skills, which can be of value anywhere in the world. As you explore other opportunities, try to meet a veterinarian who is already working in your alternative career field(s) of interest; he or she can tell you what the field is like and possibly be willing to serve as a mentor.

The AVMA currently recognizes 22 specialty organizations that include 41 distinct clinical specialties in veterinary medicine. Many internship (~1 year) and residency (~3 years) programs exist that can prepare you for board certification in one of these specialties. Or perhaps you may be interested in another graduate degree such as a masters or PhD in public health, epidemiology, bioengineering, entomology, environmental sciences, etc. Completing a graduate degree can enhance your marketability for an alternative career. The US military, state/federal government, and industry offer job opportunities with good salaries and benefits, as well as opportunities to travel and gain experience overseas. Some of these employers will pay for the education leading to a graduate degree and residencies. Finally, the military reserves can allow you to proudly serve your country while continuing to work in practice or other career track.

Kudos to Mentors

As I drafted this chapter, I compiled an exhaustive list of the awesome folks who served as major mentors in my life. When I finished, I was stunned to find that my list included more than 70 people whom I considered significant mentors in my life, and at least a hundred more who provided mentorship. My career has been quite varied, including working in private practice and academia; serving as an officer of local, state, national, and international associations and organizations; becoming involved in global veterinary medicine and public health; consulting and building capacity in developing countries; and serving on active and reserve military duty. No doubt, this illustrates how important mentors have been throughout my life and career, and I encourage everyone to do this exercise!

I am eternally indebted to these compassionate and generous people who took precious time out of their own busy lives to support, encourage, and guide the development of my career. I also cherish that, in addition to being mentors, almost all became lifelong colleagues and friends—such a gift! To be sure, I would not have been successful without the commitment of these people who believed in me when I sometimes did not believe in myself.

Mentors will play an important role in your career and life. Remember to thank the mentors who helped and supported you along the way.

Further Reading

- Bliss M. *William Osler: A Life in Medicine.* Oxford University Press; 1999.

- Bryan CS. *Osler: Inspirations from a Great Physician,* 1st ed. Oxford University Press; 1997.

- Cushing H. *The Life of Sir William Osler,* Vol. I and II, 2nd Impression Ed., Oxford University Press; 1925.

- Herriot J. *All Creatures Great and Small.* Open Road Media; 2011.

CHARACTER

THE IMPORTANCE OF CHARACTER

W. Ron DeHaven, DVM, MBA

"I care not what others think of what I do, but I care very much about what I think of what I do! That is character!"

–Teddy Roosevelt

Ever mindful of the tremendous privilege it is to be in the veterinary profession, I am reminded of my favorite quote from Teddy Roosevelt: *"Far and away the best prize that life has to offer is the chance to work hard at work worth doing."* Regardless of the specific discipline you pursue within our profession, you will have the opportunity to earn this prize every day of your professional career. Because of the efforts of veterinarians who have come before you, veterinary medicine is among the most trusted and respected of all professions. We enjoy this high public regard, not just because of the work we do, but for the manner in which we do it. The way we function as veterinarians is a reflection of the noble character of our profession—and the character of the individuals who are part of it.

What Is Character?

The *Merriam-Webster Dictionary* defines character as "the complex of mental and ethical traits marking and often individualizing a person, group, or nation." There are many beliefs about the most important traits that form one's character, and perhaps those traits are best captured in the seven classical virtues of antiquity. The four cardinal virtues are wisdom, justice, temperance, and courage (described by Plato in *The Republic*). The three transcendent virtues are faith, hope, and love (described by St. Paul in First Corinthians, Chapter 13).

In practice, good character is as simple as living by the Golden Rule in our day-to-day lives. Given the quality and rigor of veterinary education in the United States, I do not doubt that you have the requisite knowledge and, with experience, the technical competence to deliver quality veterinary medical care. But just as importantly, good character means having the wisdom, fortitude, and ethical values to do the right thing under the most difficult circumstances—even when no one else will know what you did or didn't do. Good character means having compassion and kindness of heart, not only for the animals we serve but also for their owners. No doubt a key motivator for most of us going to veterinary school was a genuine love for animals. But shortly after graduation, if not before, we realize that it is the combination of love for and caring about both animals and people that ultimately determines our relative success in whatever type of practice we find ourselves.

More Than Regulation

Early in my career with the US Department of Agriculture's Animal & Plant Health Inspection Service (APHIS), I was field Veterinary Medical Officer stationed in Kentucky and my work primarily focused on the agency's bovine brucellosis eradication program. During this time, I dealt with over 400 brucellosis-infected herds and their owners. One such herd was particularly memorable. The farm was a true "mom and pop" operation with row crops, a tobacco patch, and 40 purebred Jersey cows. The family matriarch and my primary point of contact was Mrs. Peale, who put her heart and soul into the farm, and most especially, her dairy cows. While important as the main source of income for her and her family, these gentle cows were much more to Mrs. Peale. They were her life, and she was as attached to them as most dog and cat owners are to their pets. Unlike the typical beef cattle herd where the animals are a commodity, Mrs. Peale knew every one of her cows by name and personality.

Sadly, in the course of epidemiological tracing and testing, we found brucellosis in Mrs. Peale's dairy herd. This meant we had to test the herd every month or two, and positive animals had to be branded and sent to slaughter. Collecting blood samples for brucellosis testing was typically done after the morning milking and chores, and Mrs. Peale always insisted that my colleagues and I stay for the noon-time dinner, although I suspect that accepting a meal from a "regulated party" was against some agency policy.

At first, I thought Mrs. Peale was trying to foster some good will with us, hoping that somehow sitting at the same table for a meal might influence the outcome of her testing results. But actually these meals provided us an opportunity to show her compassion and empathy for her situation. We genuinely felt horrible every time we had to take one of her cows. Over time, a sense of trust developed, and Mrs. Peale recognized that the regulatory program was in her best interests and that we would never take one of her cows unless it was absolutely necessary for the long-term health of her herd. There was a realization that the "enemy" was the disease we were jointly fighting, not the federal government.

By the time we were able to release Mrs. Peale's herd from quarantine, a genuine friendship had evolved. We never compromised on our regulatory oversight, but for me, this was the beginning of a deeper understanding that even the relationship between a regulatory agency and the regulated party does not have to be an adversarial one. On the contrary, much more can be accomplished when the regulatory officials work cooperatively with understanding, consideration, and compassion for the regulated parties within the framework of the regulatory program. We could have approached Mrs. Peale by drawing the regulatory "hard line" and possibly even have eventually arrived at the same outcome, but it would have been at considerable cost emotionally for all parties and created ill will for the program throughout the entire local community.

External Pressure Versus Internal Compass

Later in my government career, now as the Deputy Administrator for Veterinary Services in APHIS, we found the first domestic case of bovine spongiform encephalopathy (BSE) in December 2003. Literally overnight, our beef producers lost $4.8 billion in beef export markets, representing about 65% of the US annual beef exports. Approximately half this amount was lost beef exports to Japan and Korea. After months of intense technical negotiations to reopen these markets, Japan finally agreed to accept US beef again if we would test every animal at slaughter. We thought that Korea would quickly follow suit.

On the surface, this sounded easy enough, and the value of the market to be recovered was enormous—about $2.4 billion. But the reality was that such a testing program would have lacked any scientific merit and would have come at considerable cost, both financially and in damage to the agency's credibility. There are several key facts. First, no test can detect BSE in a live animal. BSE is confirmed by testing brain samples for the presence of the infectious agent (the abnormal form of the prion protein). The earliest point at which current tests can accurately detect BSE is 2–3 months before the animal begins to show signs, and this is a disease with a typical incubation period of 5 years or more. Hence, an animal infected as a calf will not demonstrate any clinical signs of the disease and test positive until it is 5–8 years old. Because most cattle in the United States are slaughtered at the age of 18–20 months, testing would not detect the disease even if present. Therefore, testing of slaughter-age beef cattle would not have any scientific value and would instead provide a false sense of food safety. In other words, because the animal tested negative, many would assume that products from that animal would be safe. At the time, about 35 million head of cattle were being slaughtered annually in the United States. At a per-test cost of about $30, this would mean the United States would be spending approximately $1 billion per year on testing that, at best, had no scientific or food safety value.

As you might imagine, there was intense political pressure from the beef industry to agree to this testing to reopen the market. When senior government officials were on the verge of agreeing to the testing, my supervisor and mentor, Mr. Bobby Acord, then Administrator of APHIS, resigned his position in protest. He said he could not be associated with this decision and the loss of credibility it would inflict on the agency. Mr. Acord's courageous action caused reconsideration and, ultimately, a reversal of the decision. Truly this was a profound example of scientific and professional integrity in action.

Facing Situations, Making Decisions

Although the examples above were from my career in public service, private practitioners face situations daily that challenge their professional integrity and personal character. Early in your career, the danger lies in making careless decisions that are not compatible with your personal character traits. How are you going to relate on an interpersonal level to colleagues and clients? What are your personal standards for veterinary care? How much are you willing to bend your integrity for expediency or personal gain? Your character is not something to leave to chance or decide on a whim but rather should be the outcome of internal reflection and consonant with your personal values.

Each of us has an obligation to act in a manner that upholds our own values and the standing of a highly respected profession. Again, Teddy Roosevelt said it well. *"Character, in the long run, is the decisive factor in the life of an individual and of nations alike."*

THE GOLDEN RULE AND ETHICS

Michael J. Blackwell, DVM, MPH, FNAP

"I have three personal ideals. One, to do the day's work well and not to bother about tomorrow.... The second has been to act the Golden Rule, as far as in my lay, towards my professional brethren and towards the patients committed to my care ... and the third has been to cultivate such a measure of equanimity as would enable me to bear success with humility, the affection of my friends without pride, and to be ready when the day of sorrow and grief came to meet it with the courage befitting a man."

–Sir William Osler

The Golden Rule is the principle of treating others as you wish them to treat you. It is a maxim found in most religions and cultures, and it may appear as a positive or negative injunction governing conduct.

- Treat others as you would like others to treat you.

- Do not treat others in ways that you would not like to be treated.

- What you wish upon others, you wish upon yourself.

The Golden Rule informs our judgment as we learn from our mistakes, adapt to change, and develop the capacity to forgive others as well as ourselves.

All veterinarians are expected to adhere to a progressive code of ethical conduct known as the Principles of Veterinary Medical Ethics. Our decisions are to be influenced only by the patient's welfare, client needs, and public safety. In all that we do, we are to uphold the public trust vested in the veterinary profession, avoiding conflicts of interest, or the appearance of same. Also, we are entrusted to provide competent clinical care under the terms of a veterinarian-client-patient relationship, with compassion and respect for both animal and human welfare. The practice of veterinary medicine, clinical and nonclinical, involves adherence to values and principles of conduct, individually and collectively, as a profession.

Core Values and Experience

Our beliefs and values drive our behaviors in both our professional and personal lives. Veterinarians must advocate for themselves, for their patients and clients, and for society as a whole. When advocating for multiple parties, competing priorities may surface. Understanding our core values and personal mission helps us to make sound, consistent decisions that safeguard the well-being of all parties.

Earning a degree in veterinary medicine is a measure of one's intellectual and problem-solving ability and an innate drive to succeed. These talents, when exercised with ethical principles, enable success. Those called to veterinary medicine possess another characteristic, that of being compassionate. Compassion is the ability to feel *for* another and have a desire to alleviate another's suffering. It is associated with empathy, the ability to feel *as* another.

Doctors of veterinary medicine are uniquely trained in comparative medicine, making veterinary medicine the broadest medical profession. We safeguard the health and well-being of animals, people, our environment, and our society. We must continually learn about health, how disease threatens it, and how to work with nature. What sets us apart as individuals and a profession is the unique ability to see these dynamics among multiple species. Veterinarians make objective, science-based decisions about the care provided to their patients, using evidence-based practices. Yet, being personally involved adds subjectivity. The Golden Rule and ethics influence our subjective experience. Science, law, philosophy, and spirituality form the arena in which we practice. While it is an honor to be responsible for the well-being of another, the responsibility is also heavy. Consequently, self-care is paramount. Our ability to effect healing starts with our own physical and mental wellness.

Ethical Dilemmas

Veterinarians must learn to manage ethical, or moral, dilemmas. These occur in situations when we must choose between two or more options, none of which is ethically ideal. For example, a prevalent ethical dilemma we face is when a patient needs a level of care beyond the client's ability to pay for it. Historically, veterinarians have endeavored to modify the patient's treatment plan; although we may not be able to do all that is desired, we can do something and avoid doing nothing. However, providing less than desired care can present an ethical dilemma. A veterinarian may possess the knowledge, skills, and ability to repair and save a badly fractured limb using internal fixation. When this is not possible because the client is unable to pay for such a surgery, an amputation may be the next best thing for the patient. Amputating the limb addresses the injury, relieving pain and suffering, but leaves the patient with a deficit. Having to settle for less than the ideal is justified when, in the end, the decision safeguards life with an acceptable level of quality.

In choosing one therapeutic plan over another, it helps to stand on a firm foundation of knowledge that you are doing the best you can with the resources available. Even so, making these decisions can leave us feeling dissatisfied, made worse especially when the situation results in euthanasia over a problem that may have been treatable. Numerous instances of these circumstances can lead to compassion fatigue, burnout, and unhappiness. Therefore, we should commit to doing what we can that is in the best interest of our patient and client, given the options available.

Appreciating the limits of what we can achieve, especially when we have the capability, helps us weather the ethical and moral dilemmas inherent in the practice of veterinary medicine. Doing something to avoid not being able to help still generates satisfaction. The late great basketball coach, John Wooden, said it best, *"Success is peace of mind, which is a direct result of self-satisfaction in knowing you made the effort to become the best you are capable of becoming."*

Character develops through being tested, including through ethical dilemmas, and especially when faced with adversity and difficulty. Under these circumstances, adhering to our values and principles defines our character. Coach Wooden said, *"The true test of a man's character is what he does when no one is watching."* My dad demonstrated this every day in his mixed animal practice. He treated his patients behind closed doors with the same care as if the client was watching. Character is an outward expression of our internal compass, based on what we do each day. As Coach Wooden put it, *"Be more concerned with your character than your reputation, because your character is what you really are, while your reputation is merely what others think you are."*

Patients and Clients

We are imperfect beings in an imperfect world. Many times, clients expressed appreciation despite my limitations. They accepted when I told them that I didn't yet know what was going on with their pet, but that I would continue trying to figure it out. Clients tend to be appreciative of our efforts to help, especially when what we do is accompanied by an attitude of service. A service-minded manner exudes positivity that influences the overall client experience. My dad often remarked to me that the practice of veterinary medicine is 90% business and 10% medicine. By 90% business, he was referring to serving others, not to the bookkeeping, ordering drugs and supplies, paying employees, and managing other necessary practice activities. Clients may show up in emotional distress because of what's happening with their animal or even their personal circumstances and, consequently, may be a challenge to serve. I saw my dad demonstrate patience, forgiveness, and a determination to show respect with a service-minded manner every single day. I came to appreciate that it is in these moments when trust develops—trust that strengthens the relationship between the veterinarian and the client.

Veterinarians need to be adaptable because every client is different, as is every patient. And your ability to help your patient is inextricably linked to the client. Some clients require more "handholding" and more of our time as they struggle to understand and face what is going on with their pet. As we practice our skills, we learn to vary the expression of our values and principles to meet client needs. We need to recognize what is most important to address our client's needs—working with the client to meet them where they stand, and through service-minded communication, moving them to where we'd like them to be. Often, I had to do this when my patient was terminal and suffering, yet the client was having difficulty in letting go. At that moment, advocating for the animal required helping the client to make a decision. What and how we communicate must vary based on the client's relationship with the animal. If the animal is a close companion, our service-minded messaging will differ from that used when the client's relationship with the animal is more utilitarian or economically driven, such as with livestock.

Connections

Being a veterinarian enables us to appreciate the tapestry of life and how everything in nature is connected, from a macro- to microlevel. The animals we help depend on our advocacy but so do our clients. Pledging to use our scientific knowledge and skills for the benefit of society is a lofty and worthy calling. Lifelong learning leads to continual improvements in our professional expertise and competence. Practicing our profession conscientiously, with dignity, and in keeping with the principles of veterinary medical ethics is a noble pursuit. At the same time, we must also advocate for ourselves. Attending to our own health and well-being improves the probability of a professional life filled with joyfulness.

Being admitted to the veterinary profession is among the highest honors bestowed on someone. Absent veterinarians, the world would be more frightful and, frankly, less attractive without our spirits and presence. In the words of John Wooden, *"Do not let what you cannot do interfere with what you can do."*

Further Reading

- AVMA. Principles of veterinary medical ethics of the AVMA. Accessed Jan 10, 2021. www.avma.org/policies/principles-veterinary-medical-ethics-avma

- AVMA. The veterinarian-client-patient relationship (VCPR). Accessed Jan 10, 2021. www.avma.org/resources-tools/pet-owners/petcare/veterinarian-client-patient-relationship-vcpr

- Flew A (ed). *"golden rule"*. In: *A Dictionary of Philosophy*. St. Martin's Press; 1984:134.

- Jimenez S. "Compassion." In: Lopez S (ed). *The Encyclopedia of Positive Psychology, Vol I.* Wiley-Blackwell; 2009.

- Long AA, Sedley DN. *The Hellenistic Philosophers: Translations of the Principal Sources with Philosophical Commentary, Vol 1.* Cambridge University Press; 1987:366–367.

- Rokeach M. *The Nature of Human Values.* Free Press; 1973.

- Wooden J. John Wooden, Coach & Teacher. Accessed Jan 10, 2021. www.coachwooden.com

COMPETENCY AND CARING

Russell W. Currier, DVM, MPH, DACVPM

*"The lengthened line of learning covers fifty years,
not just one to ten."*

–Cyril O. Houle

Veterinary practice obviously deals with animal health but in a fundamental sense, the practitioner is also in the "people business." To diagnose and treat your patients, you must have a certain level of clinical competence, which in turn, serves as an umbrella for all your professional activities. Equally crucial to scientific and technical ability is the vital characteristic of caring in all your patient and client relationships.

Competency

What you learn in school will be, in a sense, outdated on graduation. In the first 5 years after graduation, the voices of distressed alumni state we should have been taught more practical techniques. In the next 5 years, the cry changes to we should have received more theory. Even later on, the word is we should have received more education on administration and how to improve relationships with coworkers and staff. This continuum is one example demonstrating that to sustain competence, you must strive to update your education continually; consider it a lifelong process. The road to success is always under construction.

Opportunities for continued education are many and varied, including learning from your personal experience, colleagues, conferences and association meetings, self-study of texts and other sources, and even from pharmaceutical representatives and other associated businesses that service and support the veterinary profession. Volunteering to serve on association committees is another excellent way to learn more about veterinary medicine and the challenges we face while also making a contribution to the betterment of our profession. Remember the final sentence of the Veterinarian's Oath: *"I accept as a lifelong obligation the continued improvement of my professional knowledge and competence."*

Caring

Although professional competence is requisite, caring rivals in importance. The wise practitioner will exercise being even-tempered with clients. Greeting your client by name, making eye contact, shaking hands sincerely, and starting with a few questions in your first encounter are excellent techniques to develop a solid relationship. So, while you may want to completely focus on the dog, cat, horse, or other animal, realize that the owner is at the other end of the leash or lead. Treat each client as if he or she is the most important person you have encountered all day. Ask questions—and then be sure to listen carefully. People have one mouth but two ears, so resolve to not only hear their conversation but also listen to the content. Be aware of your body language and mannerisms because clients—and their pets—will pick up on them. Develop a proper "pet-side manner" by understanding and respecting the human-animal bond.

Avoid anger and hostilities because it is impossible to win an argument. If a clinical encounter results in a guarded prognosis or some distressing development, you must do your best and comfort always. You never know what a client's life is like or what he or she has been through that day, that week, or that month. Be sure to provide a chair for the client to sit down and have a box of facial tissue close by. Show you care.

Developing an Effective "Pet-Side Manner"

Dr. William McCulloch, one of the founders of the Delta Society (currently Pet Partners), lists the following characteristics that are typically exhibited by veterinarians who understand and respect the human-animal bond.

- *Empathetic:* Respect the client's feelings because they may differ from your own.
- *Patient:* Allow time for clients to make difficult decisions, especially if euthanasia is being considered.*
- *Even-tempered:* Deal calmly with a client's emotions. People in crisis situations may react angrily; do not take a distraught client's anger personally.
- *Reassuring:* Alleviate a client's guilt over an animal's illness or injury, while continuing to validate the client's strong bond with his or her pet.
- *Attentive:* Be eager to listen to what the client has to say. Client education is usually better served by answering questions than by lecturing.

*Editor's Note: This applies not only to pets but also to animals for food production when herd or flock depopulation may be required.

A Postscript

Any discussion of caring must include mention of the human-animal bond and the recognition that human health is inextricably linked to animal health and interactions. For example, the act of petting a dog has been shown to lower blood pressure and reduce stress. Likewise, regularly walking a dog exercises the pet and the owner, having a salutary effect on the health of both. The Delta Society was established in 1977 to promote these concepts and confers awards annually to worthy individuals who promote the human-animal bond.

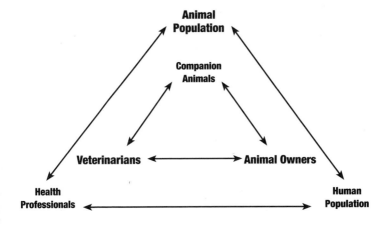

The Delta Society's triangular symbol emphasizes the human health role of the veterinarian. Points of the inner triangle connect the veterinarian to clients and patients. On the outer triangle, the veterinarian is pictured as a "health professional" related to both human and animal populations.

Further Reading

- Houle C. The lengthened line. *Perspect Biol Med.* 1967;11(1):37–51.

- McCulloch MJ. The Veterinarian in the Human-Health Care System. In: McCullough L (ed), *Implication of History and Ethics to Medicine— Veterinary and Human.* Texas A&M University Press; 1978:53–68.

- McCulloch W. The human/companion animal bond: vital topic in veterinary education. *Norden News.* Summer 1982:4–19.

SCIENTIFIC AND MORAL COURAGE AND FORTITUDE

**COL (Ret) Jerry Jaax, DVM, DACLAM, and
COL (Ret) Nancy Jaax, DVM, DACVP**

*"Success is not final, failure is not fatal: it is the courage
to continue that counts."*

–Winston S. Churchill

Courage and fortitude are linked traits and social constructs that have been universally admired and celebrated since classical antiquity. They remain important character attributes indispensable to productive, meaningful, and well-rounded lives. Moral courage, fortitude, and integrity are important pillars of our vocation and fundamental to those who aspire to professional success and fulfillment. For those veterinarians who chose academic, regulatory, military, or scientific and research careers, there can be a unique spectrum of challenges to face that require scientific and moral courage and fortitude. Examples of physical, moral, and ethical challenges might be acute, requiring momentary resolution, or they may be issues inherent in expectations for your position and persist through decades of a professional career.

During the 4th and 5th century BC, Aristotle and other Greek philosopher–physicians investigated anatomical differences and similarities of various animals—the first recorded instances of comparative biology and medicine. More recently, veterinary personnel have been essential participants in the highly regulated and complex domain of animal-based research and testing; their efforts seek expanded knowledge and development of viable countermeasures for significant human and veterinary diseases and conditions. Veterinarians with specialty and/or PhD training in pathology, laboratory animal medicine, toxicology, physiology, molecular biology, pharmacology, and virology are those in our profession most typically engaged in biomedical animal-based research. The challenges faced in these less traditional veterinary roles are certainly relevant to all in our profession, regardless of career path.

Emerging Infectious Disease Response:
The Reston Ebola Outbreak (1989–1990)

As a notable case study, the Reston Ebola outbreak was an international emerging infectious disease crisis that highlights some of the ethical, scientific, moral, and dangerous challenges and dilemmas that can occur for veterinarians engaged in biomedical research, experimentation, and emergency response. This significant event resulted in a 1994 *New York Times* bestseller by Richard Preston and a 2019 National Geographic Miniseries, both called "The Hot Zone."

In 1967, African green monkeys imported from Uganda for polio vaccine production transmitted a previously unknown fatal hemorrhagic fever to laboratory workers (25% mortality) in Marburg, Germany, and in Yugoslavia. The first filovirus, genus *Marburg,* was identified as the causative agent. In 1976 and 1979, another novel filovirus identified as Ebola virus caused several highly fatal outbreaks of hemorrhagic fever in people in Zaire and Sudan (60%–90% mortality). Unlike the 1967 Marburg outbreaks, the *Zaire ebolavirus* and *Sudan ebolavirus* strains had no known zoonotic connection. In response to a new human Marburg case in 1975 in South Africa, the US Public Health Service instituted a mandatory 30-day quarantine period for all imported nonhuman primates to counter the risk of introducing Marburg or other possible zoonoses to the United States. The natural history, reservoir, and pathogenesis of both Marburg and Ebola were unknown.

In accordance with its mission of biodefense against potential biowarfare and serious public health diseases, a small cadre of multidisciplinary scientists had maintained a sporadic filovirus research program at the US Army Medical Research Institute of Infectious Diseases (USAMRIID) at Ft. Detrick, Maryland. In the decade before the Reston Ebola outbreak, the USAMRIID filovirus research program involved veterinary scientists and collaborators who worked in high-consequence pathogen research in Biosafety Level 4 (BSL-4) biocontainment suites. During the 1980s, these veterinary officers worked with no fanfare in virtual anonymity on highly infectious filoviruses that were highly lethal and for which no vaccine, treatment, or other countermeasures were available. Handling filovirus-infected animals in BSL-4, performing pathogenesis research through repetitive in vivo blood and tissue sampling, and performing full-body necropsies of *Zaire ebolavirus*–infected animals are arguably among the most hazardous activities performed in veterinary medicine.

In late 1989, a shipment of *Cynomolgus* sp macaques imported from the Philippines and in quarantine in Reston, Virginia, broke with a fatal hemorrhagic fever syndrome. The preliminary diagnosis was simian hemorrhagic fever, a deadly non-zoonotic viral disease of macaques, and asymptomatic disease of some other monkeys. Tissues were sent to USAMRIID, where scientists confirmed the presence of simian hemorrhagic fever, and—unexpectedly—also discovered co-infection with Ebola virus.

The discovery of Ebola-infected monkeys, and presumably infected animal care workers in the quarantine facility in the heavily populated greater Washington DC area, was an unprecedented public health crisis that sparked an emergency multiagency and international response. In the face of daunting regulatory and legal questions, USAMRIID Commander, Colonel David Huxsoll, DVM, PhD, courageously directed that the Institute mount an aggressive and unparalleled response to the outbreak. The critical action to devise and execute a response to the nearly 500 monkeys infected or exposed to Ebola in the quarantine facility fell to the USAMRIID Veterinary Medicine Division (VMD).

Once preliminary planning was complete, a USAMRIID emergency response team (consisting of Army laboratory animal veterinarians and animal care technicians with training and experience working with monkeys) proceeded to the Reston facility. VMD personnel implemented the novel emergency operational response plans and safety protocols for the Ebola-infected monkeys and premises.

The outbreak presented extraordinary and unique challenges for researchers, planners, and responders:

- **Team selection:** VMD personnel were interviewed and carefully informed of the mission and its significant hazards. Voluntary participation was nearly unanimous despite the lack of BSL-4 experience.

- **Safety and efficacy of personal protective equipment:** The racal suits (protective suits with positive-pressure, HEPA-filtered respirator hoods) were thought to provide protection against aerosol pathogens but were easily torn and not designed to work around sharp edges or to grasp defensive or biting animals.

- **Severe environmental conditions:** The facility HVAC unit failed early in the operation, and the ambient temperature soared to 90°F. These extreme conditions made working with and caring for the animals even more challenging. In addition, it caused extreme discomfort and fatigue for the soldiers wearing the racal suits, making the possibility of mistakes and exhaustion a constant concern.

- *Animal welfare:* Maintaining adequate veterinary care and husbandry for the hundreds of research animals in the facility for nearly a week was logistically and physically demanding. Euthanizing hundreds of animals was dangerous, exhausting, and emotionally distressing for personnel whose professional career and technical training were focused on providing optimal care.

- *Lack of squeeze cages:* Approximately 40% of the monkey cages were not fitted with a squeeze mechanism, an important feature for safe animal handling. Use of an emergency technique devised for catching the monkeys was challenging and extremely hazardous.

- *Regulatory concerns:* Daunting regulatory and legal challenges abounded throughout the chain of command. Colonel David Huxsoll courageously supported the unprecedented actions undertaken by members of USAMRIID response teams during the crisis. For example, this included authorization to transport suspected filovirus-infected cadavers from the quarantine facility across the Maryland–Virginia state line before formal approval from state and federal regulatory agencies. Some of these decisions had the potential to be career ending; moving forward with these actions in the face of existing regulations embodied tremendous moral courage.

Ultimately, the mission was accomplished: The cadaver remains were safely, discreetly, and efficiently transported to Virginia for appropriate disposal with no exposure or illness of anyone involved.

Operation "Desert Steed" (1990–1998)

In the ramp-up for Operation Desert Storm in Kuwait, intelligence indicated that weaponized botulinum toxin could pose a serious threat to unprotected coalition forces. Years earlier, Colonel George Lewis, DVM, PhD, had performed novel postdoctoral "proof of concept" research for production of botulinum hyperimmune sera in an American Thoroughbred racehorse named First Flight. Based on this groundbreaking preliminary work, USAMRIID VMD and Toxicology Division immediately launched an extensive emergency project, internally coined Operation "Desert Steed." VMD procured horses; constructed project-appropriate barns, holding areas, and a despeciation laboratory; and hyperimmunized 100 horses against all 7 known serotypes of botulinum toxin and despeciated the sera (ie, a process to remove the animal-specific proteins).

Hyperimmunization required repeated hypodermic injection of the horses, eventually with syringes containing toxin at a dose of up to 10,000 times the human LD_{50}. Several of these botulinum serotypes had no known countermeasure or vaccine, making the physical act of injecting stanchioned horses an extremely dangerous activity. Colonel David Franz, DVM, PhD, a co-investigator on the project, chose to perform the thousands of injections entirely on his own, thereby eliminating substantial, possibly deadly, risk for other members of the research team.

Desert Storm was over before the project yielded despeciated botulinum antitoxin. However, Desert Steed antitoxin was subsequently used to successfully treat fatal outbreaks of neonatal botulism in the Middle East. Desert Steed was a spectacular scientific, logistical, and managerial success, demonstrating extreme courage and professional determination by numerous USAMRIID and Department of Defense veterinary scientists and technicians.

A Final Note

While the Reston Ebola response and the Desert Steed project exemplify scientific, moral, and physical courage by veterinarians, these dramatic and compelling illustrations are by no means isolated occurrences. They are analogous to the courage of veterinarians who serve bravely in armed conflict zones, work in areas of endemic infectious disease, and take on other dangerous assignments. These veterinarians all provide a proud legacy of service, courage, and fortitude for members of our diverse profession.

USAMRIID Veterinary Personnel Involved in the Reston Ebola Outbreak and/or Early Ebola Pathogenesis Research

Colonel David Huxsoll, USAMRIID Commander
Colonel Jerry Jaax, Chief of the Veterinary Medical Division
Colonel Nancy Jaax, Chief of the Pathology Division

Sergeant First Class Tom Amen
Major Steve Denny
Bill Gibson
Merle Gibson
Major Mark Haines
Major Martha Haines

Lieutenant Colonel Tony Johnson
Staff Sergeant Kurt Klages
(later DVM)
Colonel Jim Moe
Fred Murphy, DVM, PhD
Major Nate Powell
Lieutenant Colonel Ron Trotter

Further Reading

• Cantoni D, Hamlet A, Michaelis M, et al. Risks posed by Reston, the forgotten Ebolavirus. mSphere. 2016;1(6):e00322–16.

• Ebola (Ebola Virus Disease). Centers for Disease Control and Prevention, Oct 2017. Accessed Jan 10, 2021. www.cdc.gov/vhf/ebola/index.html

• Preston R. The Hot Zone: *The Terrifying True Story of the Origins of the Ebola Virus.* Anchor Books; 1999.

• Rollin PE, Williams RJ, Bressler DS, et al. Ebola (subtype Reston) virus among quarantined nonhuman primates recently imported from the Philippines to the United States. *J Infect Dis.* 1999;179:S108–S114.

KNOWLEDGE AND WISDOM

John Herbold, DVM, MPH, PhD, DACVPM, DACAW, FACE, FNAP

"A smart person knows what to say.
A wise person knows whether to say it or not."

–Anonymous

Most of us would define our journey through veterinary training as the accumulation of scientific knowledge—learning and comprehending specific vocabulary, facts, information, skills, procedures, and more. Later, in the clinical setting, we learn to apply that knowledge base to diagnose and treat an animal with a specific presentation or condition. We gain additional insight from watching our mentors' approach and from managing our own cases.

Wisdom is more of a philosophical concept. It is said that life experiences (especially bad experiences) engender wisdom. Does that mean that individuals early in their career lack wisdom? I don't think so. Depending on circumstances, we are all at different points on the knowledge and wisdom scales. The journey from acquiring adequate "knowledge" to developing "wisdom" is complex.

Applying Your Education

As doctors of veterinary medicine, we all must strive to gain greater knowledge and to apply it wisely. Depth of knowledge and application of wisdom are both needed as we travel on our lifetime journey in veterinary medicine. All of medicine, veterinary and human alike, is often described as both a science and an art.

Granted, we immerse ourselves in gaining a firm foundation of scientific knowledge. But I believe the art component is more closely tied to wisdom. I can equate our professional abilities to those of artisans—skilled workers who make things by hand, often trained under an apprenticeship system. That's us! We use all our senses to diagnose, assess, ameliorate, treat, and prevent disease states in our patients, whether they be individual animals, herds, or flocks. Sir William Osler, a physician deemed the father of modern medicine, emphasized the need to apply scientific knowledge in the clinical setting: *"He who studies medicine without books sails an uncharted sea, but he who studies medicine without patients does not go to sea at all."*

The Inevitability of Change

Be prepared for a professional lifetime of change and unforeseen challenges. You have been well trained for it, but you must also be prepared. Clinical practice is the launch pad for most of us, after which a wide variety of specializations and applications may follow. Not to be trite, but *"...if the only tool you have is a hammer, you treat everything as if it were a nail."* A similar expression applied specifically to medicine and surgery is *"the surgeon always reaches for the scalpel."* However, much of the knowledge gained in your training, the procedures taught, your professional interests, and the sociocultural setting in which you work will evolve over time.

A couple of years after I graduated from Texas A&M College of Veterinary Medicine in 1969, Venezuelan equine encephalitis (VEE) swept through Mexico into south Texas, potentially decimating the fledgling "horse racing" industry. A vaccine developed by the Department of Defense for use in people (biological warfare defense) was released to the US Department of Agriculture for veterinarians to immunize horses. At the time, I had the knowledge to vaccinate horses against VEE, but it was not until several years later that I had the wisdom to recognize the significance of potential "dual usage" of vaccines.

In another example, the veterinary profession was slow to recognize the sociological shift in the 1950s that took exception to the mass euthanasia of "stray" pets as a control measure for rabies outbreaks in cats and dogs. It was the questioning minds of a new generation of veterinarians that challenged what had been established public health practice at the time to effect a better method for rabies prevention and control with greatly improved vaccines and widespread vaccination programs.

The animal welfare movement in the United States traces its origins to work horses in New York City and Boston in the late 1800s and early 1900s. Small animal practice emerged in the 1930s as the country became more urbanized. Veterinary public health was formalized within the Centers for Disease Control after World War II. In the 1950s, the growth of corporate agriculture and animal husbandry led to the waning of rural mixed practice. In the 1960s, laboratory animal medicine developed, along with amazing advances in biomedical science. Corporate ownership of private veterinary practices became prevalent in the late 1990s.

Change will occur. Change never stops. Osler said, *"Live neither in the past nor in the future, but let each day's work absorb your entire energies, and satisfy your widest ambition."* That should be your mantra as you polish your skills to apply the art, science, and practice of veterinary medicine. If you remain alert to the lessons found in each day's work, change will bring you greater wisdom.

A Lifelong Journey

As you prepare for a lifetime of active involvement in the practice of veterinary medicine, take pleasure and comfort in pursuing the everyday satisfaction of "doing good" in a rewarding profession.

Do not ask your children
  to strive for extraordinary lives.
Such striving may seem admirable,
  but it is the way of foolishness.
Help them instead to find the wonder
  and the marvel of an ordinary life.
Show them the joy of tasting
  tomatoes, apples and pears.
Show them how to cry
  when pets and people die.
Show them the infinite pleasure
  in the touch of a hand.
And make the ordinary come alive for them.
  The extraordinary will take care of itself.

Source: Martin W. *The Parent's Tao Te Ching: Ancient Advice for Modern Parents.* Da Capo Lifelong Books; 1999.

Further Reading

- Bryan CS. The Virtues in Medicine. In: *A Hound Dog in Anderson and other Essays on Medicine and Life.* The South Carolina Medical Association; 2008:149–220.

- Bustad LK. More Than Scholars. In: *Compassion: Our Last Great Hope.* Delta Society [now Pet Partners]; 1990.

INTEGRITY, HONESTY, HUMILITY, AND KINDNESS

Daniel L. Grooms, DVM, PhD, DACVM

"Talent is God-given. Be humble. Fame is man-given. Be grateful. Conceit is self-given. Be careful."

–Coach John Wooden

The Gentle Doctor, an iconic sculpture on display at the Iowa State University College of Veterinary Medicine, was completed in 1938 by Danish-born artist Christian Petersen, the first permanent artist in residence at a US college or university. The statue portrays a veterinarian holding and comforting a sick puppy while the puppy's mother sits close by, looking up trustingly.

This statue uniquely embodies four core values that are at the soul of the veterinary profession: integrity, honesty, humility, and kindness. Core values are the central beliefs of a person, directing behavior and helping us recognize the difference between right and wrong. These

guiding doctrines are the bedrock upon which our profession was built and will remain for centuries to come.

Integrity

Integrity is adhering to strong ethical and moral principles, consistently and without compromise. *The Gentle Doctor's* upright posture with shoulders square and legs, feet and heels together, is a pose often taken by leaders or soldiers. This stance is associated with integrity, high character, and strong moral principles. Integrity is a foundational value, much like the strong legs and feet of *The Gentle Doctor*, on which other values are built.

Integrity as a veterinarian is vitally important. Without it, the trust that colleagues, staff, clients, and even patients have in you would be nearly impossible. The trust that society has in veterinarians is built on the integrity and actions of all in our profession.

Integrity is being uncompromising about doing the right thing regardless of the circumstances, the pressures, the rewards (or lack thereof), and the consequences. This was eloquently captured by Abraham Lincoln: *"I desire to so conduct the affairs of the administration that if, at the end, when I come to lay down the reins of power, I have lost every other friend on earth, I shall have at least one friend left — and that friend shall be down inside of me."*

I remember once being asked to perform a surgical procedure that would enhance the appearance of an animal by modifying a potentially genetic defect. I agreed, but only if at the same time, the animal could be sterilized. The client walked out the door, but I knew that I had done the right thing.

Honesty

Honesty is an attribute of moral character that means being truthful and trustworthy and that also involves being loyal, fair, and sincere. When you are honest, you present yourself genuinely and sincerely and take responsibility for your feelings and actions.

As a person of integrity, your behaviors are consistent, regardless of the situation. You are unfailingly true to yourself and others, you are who you say you are, and you speak the truth.

It is essential to understand the impact of not being honest. In the bestselling and widely acclaimed novel *The Kite Runner,* Baba has an exchange with his son Assan talking about the sin of stealing in which he says, *"When you tell a lie, you steal someone's right to the truth."* This is true whether in the context of a simple verbal exchange or in how you present yourself on a day-to-day basis. Honesty allows transactions and relationships to be built on a rock-solid foundation, making them valid and unimpeachable. The opposite creates a state of affairs that is built on sand.

The Gentle Doctor statue is quietly powerful, free of distracting overtones and unnecessary noise. Its simplicity depicts a profession built on being true and honest and dedicated to a lifetime of caring. As William Shakespeare said, *"No legacy is so rich as honesty."* A lifetime of caring for God's creatures and living life honestly is indeed a rich legacy to leave.

Humility

Humility is the quality of being humble. Both words—humility and humble—have their origin in the Latin word *humilis*, meaning "low." The bowed head and kind expression of *The Gentle Doctor* depicts total focus on caring for the patient, certainly not on self and not on the adulations that may come from an owner when the health of the puppy is restored.

Humility is widely seen as a virtue that centers on not being obsessed with one's self and not seeking to be the center of attention. Humble team members are quick to recognize the contributions of others and unlikely to seek notice for their own. They rapidly share credit, accentuate team over self, and define success as a collective rather than an individual accomplishment. We mustn't confuse humility with being self-demeaning. Rick Warren, the author of

The Purpose Driven Life, described humility this way: *"Humility is not thinking less of yourself, it's thinking of yourself less."* A truly humble person is unpretentious, unassuming, and down to earth.

Kindness

Kindness is a virtue universally associated with veterinarians. Dr. Frank K. Ramsey, an esteemed veterinary pathologist, eloquently captured many characteristics associated with kindness in his description of *The Gentle Doctor: "The Gentle Doctor...reflects concern, affection, love, and the significance of life for all of God's creatures—great and small."* As the figure portrayed in *The Gentle Doctor* compassionately looks at the tranquil puppy, the veterinarian's facial expression and hands, which are placed gently on the puppy's back, depict a kind and caring person. Likewise, it is apparent that the puppy's mother understands *The Gentle Doctor's* compassionate caring and kind nature as she gazes upward, relinquishing control of her charge to the trusted caregiver.

What is kindness? Friendliness, generosity, gentleness, warmth, and concern are words that come to mind. But kindness is more than these simple descriptive words. It is more than just being nice. It is genuinely caring for others—caring for their well-being, their success, their happiness, regardless of their background or the circumstances. It is also about caring for ourselves. If you cannot be kind and care for yourself, how can you honestly be kind to others?

Kindness is also sometimes called for in circumstances that are not always positive. For example, consider when you must say "no" to someone who asks for money to support a substance abuse or gambling habit, or something else harmful. In a professional setting, a kind veterinarian could counsel a person against owning a pet when resources are lacking, out of concern for both the person and animal's well-being. In situations such as these, "tough love" is an act of kindness. Similarly, euthanasia can, in most circumstances, be viewed as an act of kindness. Although very often heart-wrenching, euthanasia is most often performed because we care so much for the animal's quality of life and wish to relieve suffering. Carefully considering euthanasia as an act of kindness may be one way to alleviate the compassion fatigue that takes such a toll on members of our profession.

It is often said that kindness costs nothing and means everything. Genuinely caring for ourselves, our family members, our friends, our colleagues, our clients, and our patients is the ultimate act of kindness.

> *Integrity, honesty, humility, and kindness:*
> *core values so deeply entrusted to our profession.*
> *Reflect upon them, study them, live them.*

Further Reading

- Bliss PL. *Christian Peterson Remembered.* Iowa State University Press; 1986.
- Hosseini K. *The Kite Runner.* Riverhead Books; 2003.
- Iowa State University College of Veterinary Medicine Art. Accessed Jan 10, 2021. https://vetmed.iastate.edu/about/history/college-art
- Johnson LC. The origin and legacy of Christian Petersen's Gentle Doctor. *Vet Herit.* 2016;39(2):54–59.
- The story of the Gentle Doctor. *Iowa State Univ Vet.* 1982;44(2):11. Accessed Jan 10, 2021. https://lib.dr.iastate.edu/iowastate_veterinarian/vol44/iss2/11
- Warren R. *The Purpose Driven Life.* Zondervan; 2012.

CONFIDENCE, TRUST, HOPE, AND OPTIMISM

Donald L. Noah, DVM, MPH, DACVPM

"Optimism is the faith that leads to achievement; nothing can be done without hope and confidence."

–Helen Keller

My intent for this chapter is to be a confidence-builder and a reminder of how well educated and valuable you are to your beneficiaries, both four- and two-legged. I believe this applies to anyone who has successfully progressed to this point in the pursuit of becoming a veterinarian.

Confidence

None of us are immune from the "imposter syndrome.'" Each one of us has had thoughts that everyone else is better prepared, smarter, or more capable than ourselves. Believe me, this is rarely true! Fortunately, there are effective defense mechanisms against this insidious concept. First, hone your critical thinking abilities and apply them in your professional endeavors. Your professors and mentors have provided you with a vast amount of knowledge. It is up to you to be resilient and persistent in how you apply it.

I'll tell you about a somewhat embarrassing situation I experienced within the first year after graduating from veterinary college. I was on a farm call and had just treated a cow for mild neurologic symptoms (for which I presumptively diagnosed, and treated for, listeriosis). As I was putting my equipment back in the truck, the farmer's wife asked me, "When should we vaccinate our goats for overeating disease?" I mentally froze and my mind shifted into a higher gear because I had no idea what she was talking about. Of course, I knew about enterotoxemia due to *Clostridium perfringens* types C and D, but I was not familiar with this lay term. Rather than admit to the possibility (probability?) of looking like an idiot, I took a bit of a risk and asked, "When did you vaccinate them the last time?" in hopes that her answer would provide a clue. She replied that it had been almost a year, so she thought they were about due. I heaved an internal sigh of relief and said that I would be out the following week to get that job done. When I was back to the clinic, replenishing the truck, I asked my dad (my first employer and incredible life mentor) about overeating disease and he said, "Oh, that's just enterotoxemia. You have several vials of vaccine in your truck." I was happy to learn this bit of lay language and made a mental note to not charge the client a trip charge when I returned to administer the vaccine. This represents a second bit of armor against feeling like an imposter. Becoming familiar with general or local lay terms for common veterinary maladies and using a judicious mixture of these lay terms and technical terms can be a very effective way to exhibit both common sense and professional knowledge.

An additional important point regarding confidence is matching your professional competence with the expectations of your employer—and those of your clients. In a 2003 article in the *Canadian Veterinary Journal*, the then-president of the Canadian Veterinary Medical Association, Dr. J. Lofstedt, identified the mismatch in these respective expectations as a significant source of dissatisfaction and discord between new graduates and their employers. In the past, I believe this certainly has been true. As I mentioned, my father was a veterinarian and he employed many new graduates over the course of his long career in mixed animal practice. He frequently claimed that it took between 6 and 12 months for a new graduate to actually start making money for the practice. (I always remembered that… but never had the guts to ask how long it took me!) Fortunately for you, a lot has changed in veterinary education since that article was published. Nearly all North American veterinary colleges have increasingly focused on graduating "day-one-ready" veterinarians. This means you are significantly better prepared to financially and professionally contribute to your practices far earlier than new graduates did in years past.

It is not enough, though, to just be better prepared; you also have to act better prepared. After graduating, every diagnosis you make, every single surgery you perform, will be the first time you've ever done it in the real world. Never shy away from doing something for the first time…even if you do not fully believe you have the skills to do it. This does not mean that you shouldn't ever refer a complicated case, but you should be willing to push yourself to expand the limits of your medical and surgical capabilities. As a long-time member of a state veterinary licensing board's investigative committee, I can tell you that state boards almost never reprimand veterinarians for reaching a bit above their professional comfort zone, especially when client funds or geographic proximity precludes specialty referral.

Trust

As you can see in the following bar chart, the general public places great trust in you as a veterinarian. That trust is not misplaced. It has been earned over many decades of valuable service by those who have come before you. On a much more personal level, however, maintaining that trust by you as an individual veterinary practitioner is critical to your credibility and, thus, to your livelihood. Each and every client who places the future of their beloved pet or valued herd in your hands is relying on you to be the trusted professional they expect you to be. That means applying critical thinking, making correct diagnoses, prescribing efficacious medications, and performing competent surgical procedures. Just as importantly, something that seems sadly inapparent with an overreliance on social media, it also means being a respectable, responsible citizen. One they need you to be in times of need, one they may wish they were in life, and one they want their kids to look up to. That also means, from the perspective of the society in which you live and practice, you are always "on." Let me repeat that: *You are always on*. When you are at a social event, a music concert, or even a private event, your actions and behaviors, as well as your dress, grooming, and personal hygiene, will reflect on your professional life.

Fortunately, you do not have to look far for guidance on earning professional and societal trust. Each of you has had one or several mentors who influenced you from past to present. Ask yourself:

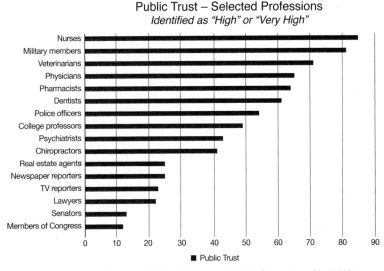

Public Trust – Selected Professions
Identified as "High" or "Very High"

Data source: Gallop News Poll. Honesty/Ethics in Professions. Accessed Jan 12, 2021.
https://news.gallup.com/poll/1654/honesty-ethics-professions.aspx

What did you admire about them? How did they behave in private and in public? How did others perceive them? The answers to these honest questions will give you significant clues and insights into your own behavior.

Just as the public places inherent trust in you as a veterinarian, which I have every confidence that you will continue to earn and enhance, you should feel great trust in the knowledge given you by those who educated you, provided you with incomparable opportunity, and perhaps even employed you. This includes your parents and grandparents, your teachers from grade school through veterinary college, perhaps historical scientists and even certain political and sports figures. You are a product of the best of each of them; rely on their lessons to guide you so you can ultimately trust yourself.

Hope

It is a stark reality that not every animal presented to you will experience a positive medical outcome. Bad outcomes come with the territory, although they are very rarely the expectation. Your clients will come to you, even when they subliminally feel an alternative truth, in the hope that you can and will change the course of their animal's future. Sometimes you will. When you do, good for you. When you cannot, however, all is not lost. Even when defeated by the vagaries of time and inevitable pathology, you can maintain not only personal sanity but also societal trust by means of your professionalism, demeanor, humanity, and promise of future hope. Dr. William Osler, a visionary in both the medical and veterinary professions, wrote: *"Once gain the confidence of a patient and inspire him with hope, and the battle is half won."* Further, he echoed Galen: *"Confidence and hope do more good than physic [medication]—'he cures most in whom most are confident.'"*

Optimism

I also wish to convey a message of enduring optimism, regarding both your personal choice of profession as well as the future of the entire veterinary profession. Given that much of my career has been spent in public health practice, I have often been asked, "Do you ever wish you had gone to medical school instead of veterinary college?" My answer has never wavered: No! Would I have made more money as a physician? Almost assuredly. Would my status in society be higher? Perhaps. My personal yardstick for self-actualization, however, has always rested on how I felt about the changes I made in the lives of others, whether they were my animal patients, my patients' owners, my students, or the populations I hope I enhanced through disease investigations and subsequent interventions.

The veterinary profession remains a "wide open" profession in that we have only just begun to stretch its boundaries. When my father graduated from veterinary college (Ohio State, 1966), public health practice was a mere shape in the fog. Since my own graduation (Ohio State, 1985), veterinarians have become governors, US senators, and even astronauts. We've worked in every sector of American society and proven ourselves worthy against every type of societal adversity. One of the reasons why I so enjoy teaching veterinary public health is that it represents an aspect of veterinary medicine that *nobody* comes to school for. Admit it, you did not aspire to become a veterinarian so you could investigate human disease outbreaks, work at the Central Intelligence Agency to counter international biological weapons programs, or reduce the mortality rate among our military members in Iraq and Afghanistan. Yet this profession has allowed me to pursue those novel opportunities. Probably many of you know exactly why you came to veterinary school and exactly what you want to do with your degree for the rest of your life. If that remains true, absolutely good for you. But unless I miss my guess, many of you will experience a mid-career curiosity for something else. Fortunately, as the One Health concept continues to grow and open more and more opportunities, that "something else" is bounded only by your imagination.

I end with an anecdote that is my personal version of something that surely will happen to each and every one of you. It will define that very first moment when you realize that you have been accepted as a *true* veterinarian, knowing that you have earned the respect that you looked forward to accompanying your professional knowledge and stature. In our mixed animal practice, we had several clients who were known for being…let's just say unforgiving of what they felt were "new graduate failings." Before I joined the practice, one dairy client in particular had ordered at least two new graduates off his farm with the threat of bodily harm should they ever return. For at least two years, I lived in fear of that man. I knew he had been a US Marine in World War II, had stormed the beaches of several enemy-held positions in the Pacific, and had undoubtedly killed people with his bare hands. Every time I was on his farm, I made sure I was on my "A game," and I was more careful than with any other client. One night, he called our practice to treat a cow with persistent proud flesh (a rare malady for a dairy cow), and I was on call. After treating the cow, which was rather straightforward, he asked me the dreaded question, "Doc, are you in a hurry?" Large animal practitioners live in fear of the "while you're here" question because it tends to blow out your schedule for that day or evening. Regardless, I replied that I had time for whatever he had in mind. He asked me to wait a moment and disappeared from the milk house into the blowing snow. After several minutes, he returned with a crystal decanter and two cut-glass tumblers on a silver platter. Keep in mind, we're both wearing coveralls, jackets, gloves, and boots—none of which were very clean. Anyway, after closing the door and shaking off the snow, he said that he had a bottle of decent whiskey and wanted to know if I'd like a "wee bit." It suddenly occurred to me that, as a recent widower, he was a lonely man…and that, somehow, he had inexplicably chosen me to share some time and drink with him. At that instant, I knew two things: First, I would have spent the entire night in that milk house with him. Second, I knew I had finally come to age as a veterinarian.

You will have your version of that true story. Enjoy it.

Further Reading

- Honesty/ethics in professions. Gallup, Inc. Accessed Jan 10, 2021. https://news.gallup.com/poll/1654/honesty-ethics-professions.aspx

- JAMA 100 Years Ago. Medicine of the nineteenth century (editorial). *JAMA.* 2001;285(5):511. (Reprint of *JAMA.* 1901;36:327–328.)

- Lofstedt J. Confidence and competence of recent veterinary graduates — Is there a problem? *Can Vet J.* 2003;44(5):359–360.

- Osler W. The reserves of life. *St. Mary's Hosp Gaz.* 1907;13:95–98.

LOVE AND SERVICE

Lawrence A. Busch, DVM, MDiv

"Love in order to serve medicine: To serve the art of medicine as it should be served, one must love his fellow man."

–Sir William Osler

What does it mean to love and serve our fellow man? All of life is a journey that is in constant flux, and we all need to find the path in which we can best serve. As I look back, my journey traversed various levels of love and service, and I identify with the following devotional post by J.D. Walt: *"I tend to live at the level of my needs and of wants-driven expectations rather than the deep seated, God-given longings of my soul.... Our needs and wants will lead us like bread crumbs to our deeper longings. Because our core longings are God-given, they can only be God-filled. ...Sound simple? It is simple. And hard. It will take... years to get it."*

St. Paul described the three theological virtues of faith, hope, and love (I Corinthians 13:13). He also offered that the greatest of the three is love. As such, love is vital to a high-quality life—love of oneself, love of others, and to be loved. Recognize that love for others must be sincere with no expectation that it will be returned... but in the long term, if practiced faithfully, love is always returned, although not always in the way we might have imagined.

I hope that sharing a few lessons I have experienced in my life's journey will help you relate more specifically to what it means to love and serve your fellow man through the healing of animals.

The Lesson of the Embryo

When I was in veterinary school, our embryology course used a human textbook. I had never spent much time on origins, either evolutionary or biblical, but studying the growth of a fetus convinced me that there had to be a Creator to engineer and oversee such intricate developments. I recognized God's handiwork and realized that on a personal level, I was *"fearfully and wonderfully made"* (Psalm 139:14). This step in my journey of love began as a friendship bond with brotherly affection, and then moved on to respect for God's creations—man and animals—and to serve Him in "dominion" healing service. Love does not exist without a relationship, and love is active, which implies service to others. This love helped me to care for my patients and clients. It helped in all my relationships in general.

The Lesson of Professional Relationships

During my time in the Epidemic Intelligence Service at the Centers for Disease Control, I investigated epidemics involving zoonotic diseases and wrote annual statistical reports on the incidence of specific zoonotic diseases in the United States. Providence was surely guiding my life, as I was assigned to the Veterinary Public Health Division in the office of the Assistant Surgeon General, where I wrote annual statistical reports on the incidence of specific zoonotic diseases in the United States. I was also a "gofer" for Dr. James H. Steele (1913–2013), who was then and still is in my memory a model for love of man, love of animals, and love for public health—in that context, a servant to all.

In the foreword to Dr. Steele's biography, Dr. George Beran noted that *"the entities and associations through which Dr. Steele worked have integrated a veterinary medical focus into essentially all of health, a focus which is becoming even more beneficial as world interactions enhance the knowledge of the inter-transmission of zoonotic and emerging diseases."* In Dr. Steele's words: *"Human and animal health are inextricably linked. They always have been. They always will be."*

In consideration of love and service, Dr. Steele's influence and contributions serve as a reminder that each of us is a vital cog in the veterinary profession and in our communities.

The Lesson of Limitations

Life is a series of challenges for everyone. At times you will find yourself puzzled, frustrated, and possibly ill prepared to determine a course of action or find a solution. It's helpful to remember the aphorism, *"To cure sometimes, to relieve often, to comfort always,"* which originated with Dr. Edward Livingston Trudeau (1848–1915), an American physician and public health pioneer who founded a tuberculosis sanatorium in the Adirondack Mountains in New York. During the limitations of an era in which antibiotics were not yet available, Dr. Trudeau worked tirelessly to establish principles for disease prevention and control. Another useful reminder in understanding and accepting our limitations with grace is the "Serenity Prayer," written by the American theologian Reinhold Niebuhr (1892–1971): *God, grant me the serenity to accept the things I cannot change, courage to change the things I can, and wisdom to know the difference.*

The Lesson of Service

I was on a dystocia call, assisting in a calving. I enjoyed being present at any birth—the sight of new life is always a reminder of the panorama of love. As I worked at the south end of this northbound cow, I began to ask myself what I would do if I left practice. A few things came to mind, but in mid-career, I was providentially guided into full-time Christian service in ordained ministry. God called me from loving and serving my fellow man's animals to directly loving and serving my fellow man.

Your Unique Journey

Each of us has a unique call to a personal journey. No two journeys are exactly alike, but love and service should and will be part of them all. My hope is that you will serve with faith and love throughout whatever journey you are called to take.

Further Reading

- Bryan CS. *Osler–Inspirations from a Great Physician.* Oxford University Press; 1997.

- Bryan CS. *A Hound Dog in Anderson and Other Essays on Medicine and Life.* Phrontistery Press; 2008.

- Carter CN, Hoobler CG. *Animal Health, Human Health, One Health: The Life and Legacy of Dr. James H. Steele,* 2009 (distributed by the University of Texas School of Public Health).

- *The Quotable Osler.* American College of Physicians; 2008.

- Walt JD. The Seedbed Daily Text. The Farm Team. Accessed April 17, 2020. seedbed.com

FAIRNESS AND SOCIAL RESPONSIBILITY

Lorin D. Warnick, DVM, PhD, DACVPM

"Truth never damages a cause that is just."

–Mahatma Gandhi

As is the case for many veterinarians, my desire to pursue veterinary medicine as a profession was sparked early in my childhood. I grew up on my family's dairy farm on the high plains of Montana, and was responsible, along with the rest of my family, for the feeding and care of dairy cattle, horses, pigs, rabbits, and farm dogs and cats. I looked forward to the visits by our local veterinarians and liked to watch them work. I was fascinated with the vet trucks outfitted with unusual equipment, medical instruments, and drawers full of medicines. The veterinarian's skills were broad; after checking for a displaced abomasum in one of our Holstein-Friesen cows, he could perform on-the-spot surgery to remove a small tumor from the foot of our dog.

In high school, I participated in a vocational education program, spending afternoons riding with our local veterinarian, Dr. John Peebles, who operated a mixed-animal practice with his brother Bill. (Dinosaur enthusiasts may recognize the name from *Maiasaura peeblesorum*, a duck-billed dinosaur species unearthed on the Peebles ranch near Choteau, Montana). This experience gave me an insider's view of a veterinarian's work, and I helped as much as possible. I assisted with cesarean surgeries on beef cows, holding the uterus as Dr. Peebles sutured the incision, with the cow munching on hay throughout. I kept newborn calves warm in the pickup cab en route to the veterinary clinic to be given intravenous fluids for dehydration. Those and many other experiences confirmed my interest in becoming a large animal clinician.

That choice led me to work as an academic clinician, as an epidemiologist studying foodborne pathogens and antimicrobial resistance, and ultimately to my current position as dean of a veterinary college. Although my career in veterinary medicine went in directions that I had not previously imagined, the lessons from the farm stayed with me. High among them was a deep sense of fairness and responsibility.

As veterinarians, we play a vital role in the health and safety of our communities and society. While it can be tempting to think our choices affect only ourselves and the patients we treat, we must remember that our impact reaches far beyond our own practice. We have the responsibility to consider the broader public good beyond our self-interest and even the immediate interest of an individual client.

The Bureau of Animal Industry

Nowhere has this truth been clearer than during the creation and work of the Bureau of Animal Industry (BAI). The agency was founded in 1884 to fight livestock diseases and was led by Cornell's first veterinary graduate, Dr. Daniel Salmon, and the physician Theobald Smith. Students of Cornell's founding professor of veterinary medicine, Dr. James Law, became the staff, including Drs. Fred Kilborne, Cooper Curtice, and V.A. Moore. The great importance of this agency, and the veterinarians who worked with it, is described in Olmstead and Rhode's book *Arresting Contagion: "The agency would make spectacular advances in both science and public policy. It is credited with creating the template for regional disease eradication that would be used around the world in fighting ... animal and human disease.... This agency evolved to overcome great obstacles, including ignorance, rampant disease denialism, constitutional impediments, knotty jurisdictional conflicts, and strong grassroots resistance. Its successes have led later generations to take these accomplishments for granted and to forget the scientific and political challenges that had to be overcome."*

Indeed, many people are unaware of the BAI and its many accomplishments during the 1900s, which included the eradication or control of major animal diseases in the United States, such as contagious bovine pleuropneumonia, foot-and-mouth disease, and bovine tuberculosis. These accomplishments required the tenacious bravery and integrity of countless veterinarians across the country. To guide the ambitious and painstaking efforts to eradicate such widespread contagious diseases of livestock, veterinarians had to face myriad hostile and often powerful groups. For example, in 1889, BAI efforts to quarantine and cull cattle suspected of having contagious bovine pleuropneumonia led to an angry, armed mob confronting the BAI and veterinarians on Long Island, New York. Then there was the "Cow War" of 1931, which, sparked by BAI efforts to eradicate bovine tuberculosis, saw hundreds of Iowa farmers challenge veterinarians sent to test cattle for this dangerous zoonotic disease. County sheriffs and Iowa National Guard personnel were activated for security. Besides irate farmers, agency veterinarians faced challenges from the meat and dairy industries. Chicago stockyard owners and meat packers resisted the type of testing and oversight the BAI required to keep food sources safe for consumption and to eliminate disease transmission. As Olmstead and Rhode describe in *Arresting Contagion*, *"Many large packers at that time opposed having scientifically trained veterinarians near their plants, and ... made statements suggesting that they did not understand or subscribe to the fundamental principles of disease control. All segments of the livestock industry—growers, dairymen, shippers, and packers— selectively denied major health threats. All fought investigating health problems and enacting effective regulations because they feared exposure might threaten consumer confidence and trade."*

Veterinarians were also up against unscrupulous cattle traders like the notorious James Dorsey of Gilberts, Illinois. He purposefully traded cattle diagnosed with tuberculosis to buyers in other states to make a profit—all under the powerful protection of the Illinois dairy industry. Unfortunately, not all veterinarians worked to stop Dorsey and his ilk. Corrupt veterinarians took money from Dorsey to sign fraudulent health certificates, claiming that sick cattle had had a negative tuberculin test. The BAI estimated that Dorsey's activities likely led to untold thousands of cases of human tuberculosis, which occurred before mandated milk pasteurization.

It is a sobering history lesson that some veterinarians aided in the spread of such a terrible and insidious zoonotic disease. I recount these events to remind you of the great responsibility that comes with taking the Veterinarian's Oath. Not only must we do no harm, but we must always practice ethically, even when a client or other interests wish us to do differently. The choices veterinarians make can affect us all and can damage both the public good and the public trust. This is as true now as it was in 1920.

The Veterinarian's Role in Responsible Antimicrobial Use

A contemporary example of veterinarians' duty in promoting the public good is our role in administering and prescribing antimicrobial drugs. Our profession has witnessed the discovery of antibiotics, their seemingly miraculous impact on human and animal disease, and, in recent decades, the emergence and spread of antibiotic resistance. As Kathrin Mohr writes in *How to Overcome the Antibiotic Crisis,* "*After the first euphoria it was quickly realized that bacteria are able to develop, acquire, and spread numerous resistance mechanisms. Whenever a new antibiotic reached the market it did not take long until scientists observed the first resistant germs."*

Along with our colleagues in human health, veterinarians must understand the factors that contribute to antibiotic resistance in human and animal settings and practice judicious antibiotic use. This includes knowing and adhering to the laws and policies governing antimicrobial drug use and following judicious use guidelines of the American Veterinary Medical Association and other professional organizations. Decreasing antimicrobial resistance is a multifactorial challenge involving human health, consumer behavior, veterinary medicine, and agricultural practices. Veterinarians contribute to solutions by promoting effective disease prevention measures, good nutrition and husbandry, and client education. Antimicrobial administration decisions for herds, flocks, and individual animals play a role, as do biosecurity measures to prevent the spread of resistant bacterial strains. The same principles developed in the early years in the BAI to combat widespread infectious disease are relevant today—whether applied to the challenge of antimicrobial resistance, to continued efforts to control or eradicate contagious diseases, or to practicing One Health principles to prevent the next pandemic.

Roles and Responsibilities from the Patient to the Public

In joining the veterinary profession, you enter a career of great importance and service to society. Besides the scientific knowledge underlying your clinical practice, you will be a communicator, an educator, and a trusted source of information for your clients. These roles are rewarding but also come with great responsibility for lifelong education, continual improvement, and ethical practice. Whether you are working in private practice, academia, biomedical research, wildlife conservation, or as a military veterinarian or a member of a public health team, your actions have far-reaching impacts. Let us apply the lessons from our profession's history and join those who are remembered for high standards of conduct.

I reflect on those early days growing up on our Montana farm, doing work that mattered, watching with fascination and appreciation the impact our local veterinarian had on our animals, and in turn, our livelihood. It was that first impression—that of someone using both technical skill and good judgment to do what's best for animals and the people relying on them—that has been the foundation for my commitment to fairness and social responsibility.

As you take this next step and join your colleagues in veterinary medicine, remember you're entering a profession that inherently invokes a higher sense of purpose and duty, not just for the individual patient under your care, but for the public good and society as a whole.

Further Reading

- Olmstead AL, Rhode PW. *Arresting Contagion: Science, Policy, and Conflicts over Animal Disease Control.* Harvard University Press; 2015.

- Stadler M, Dersch P (eds). *How to Overcome the Antibiotic Crisis: Facts, Challenges, Technologies and Future Perspectives.* Springer; 2016.

LUMINARIES IN VETERINARY MEDICINE

Howard H. Erickson, DVM, PhD

The brief biographical sketches below are of 13 individuals, 7 American and 6 international, who have made significant contributions to veterinary medicine. They are but a few of the many pioneers or luminaries in the veterinary profession.

Claude Bourgelat

Claude Bourgelat (1712–1779) was born on March 27, 1712, the son of a noble family in Lyon, France. He studied for and originally planned to practice law, but his love of horses resulted in a change of plans. In 1740, Bourgelat became the grand equerry of France and also the director of the Lyon Academy of Horsemanship, a school for young noblemen to learn equestrian arts, swordsmanship, mathematics, music, and manners.

Claude Bourgelat (1712–1779)
Source: Wellcome Images.
Wikimedia Commons,
https://commons.wikimedia.
org/wiki/File:Portrait_
of_Claude_Bourgelat_
Wellcome_L0013625.jpg

Bourgelat studied the veterinary classics of the time and learned the anatomy, physiology, and pathology of animals under the direction of two surgeons. Circa 1744, he published a *Treatise on Horsemanship,* which brought him significant recognition. In 1750, with his gifted understanding of equine husbandry, he published a book titled *Elements of Hippiartry and the New Knowledge of Equine Medicine.*

In the mid-1700s, King Louis XV was concerned about diseases in cattle, such as rinderpest. Henri Leonard Jean Baptiste Bertin, administrator of the region of Lyon from 1754 to 1757, proposed the establishment of a veterinary school in Lyon under Bourgelat's leadership. Bourgelat secured a grant from the King to do so, and the first veterinary school in the world came to be in August 1761, with the first students admitted 6 months later. Shortly after the school in Lyon was established, rinderpest plagues were suppressed. Bourgelat also investigated and was successful in eradicating an outbreak of glanders in French cavalry horses. In 1764, Bertin ordered Bourgelat to establish another veterinary school in Alfort, near Paris. Bourgelat continued to teach until he died on January 3, 1779, at age 67.

Further Reading

- Barber-Lomax JW. Claude Bourgelat. *J Small Anim Pract.* 1964;5(1):3–4.
- Larkin M. Pioneering a profession: the birth of veterinary education in the Age of Enlightenment. *J Am Vet Med Assoc.* 2011;238(1):8–11.
- Welfel SD. Doctor of donkeys: the story of Claude Bourgelat, who turned his love of equids into a medical profession. *Vet Herit.* 2019; 42(2):56–60.

Leo Bustad

Leo Bustad (1920–1998) was born in Stanwood, Washington, on January 10, 1920. He earned three degrees from Washington State College: a bachelor's in agriculture in 1941, a master's in animal nutrition in 1948, and a doctor of veterinary medicine in 1949. He earned his PhD in physiology from the University of Washington School of Medicine in 1960. Bustad was commissioned a second lieutenant in the US Army on the same day he received his bachelor's

Leo Bustad (1920–1998)
Photo courtesy of Pet Partners
(formerly Delta Society),
https://petpartners.org/

degree in 1941. He served in the infantry in World War II with combat duty in Germany, Italy, and North Africa and was a prisoner of war in a German prison camp in the Polish Corridor. Following World War II, Bustad worked at the Hanford Laboratories from 1949 to 1965, and then at the University of California–Davis, from 1965 to 1973 as director of the radiobiology laboratory and comparative oncology laboratory, working extensively with miniature swine. He returned to Washington State University (WSU), serving as Dean of the College of Veterinary Medicine from 1973 to 1983.

Bustad was one of the first to recognize the importance of the human-animal bond and was a strong advocate for pet therapy. After he retired, he devoted much of his time to the Delta Society (currently Pet Partners), of which he was a founding member. He served as director of the People-Pet Partnership Program at WSU. Bustad wrote *Animals, Aging and the Aged* and *Compassion: Our Last Great Hope,* and he was co-author of *Learning and Living Together: Building the Human-Animal Bond.*

The Washington State Veterinary Medical Association named Bustad the Outstanding Veterinarian of the Year in 1981 and bestowed him with the Distinguished Service Award in 1984. In addition, Bustad received the WSU Distinguished Alumnus Award in 1985. Bustad was a senior member of the Institute of Medicine of the National Academy of Sciences and a consultant to the Surgeon General of the US Air Force.

Further Reading

- Bustad L. *Compassion: Our Last Great Hope*. Delta Society; 1990.
- Caraher P. Leo Bustad, former WSU Dean of Veterinary Medicine, dies at age 78. *Moscow-Pullman Daily News*. September 21, 1998.
- Villalobos A. "Speaking for Spot," Dr. Nancy Kay and Dr. Leo Bustad. *Vet Pract News*. August 1, 2012.

Aleen Isabel Cust

Aleen Cust (1868–1937) was an Anglo-Irish veterinary surgeon. She was born at Cordangan Manor in Tipperary, Ireland, to a family with royal ties. She first began training as a nurse in a London hospital but quit to pursue veterinary medicine. In 1894 at the age of 26, Cust enrolled in the New Veterinary College, Edinburgh, as A.I. Custance to spare her family any embarrassment.

Cust won many medals in scholastic competition during her college years. When she was to sit for the first of her professional examinations in 1897, the Council of the Royal College of

Aleen Cust (1868–1937)
Source: *Vet Rec.* 1934
Apr 7;XIV(14):360.
Wikimedia Commons, https://
commons.wikimedia.org/wiki/
File:Aleen_Cust_portrait.jpg

Veterinary Surgeons (RCVS) declined her application. As the governing body for the RCVS, the Council defined the word "student" as "male student" and ruled that the RCVS lacked authority to admit a woman to the examination.

After her graduation in 1900, Cust returned to her native Ireland with a letter of recommendation from William Williams, principal of the New Veterinary College. Although unable to call herself a veterinarian, she worked as an assistant to William Augustine Byrne, MRCVS, in Athleague, County Roscommon, and was later named veterinary inspector to the Galway County Council. Parliament, however, cleared the final hurdle for Cust to realize her dream with passage of the Sex Disqualification (Removal) Act of 1919. Under the new law, women could no longer be barred from any profession. In 1922, Aleen Cust became the first female veterinary surgeon to be recognized by the RCVS.

Further Reading

- Ford CM. *Aleen Cust, Veterinary Surgeon: Britain's First Woman Vet.* Biopress Ltd; 1990.
- Nolan RS. Britain's first woman veterinarian. *J Am Vet Med Assoc.* 2011;238(11):1387–1388.
- Mattson K. UK celebrates 100 years of women veterinarians. *J Am Vet Med Assoc.* 2020;256(6):626.

Peter C. Doherty

Peter Charles Doherty was born on October 15, 1940, near Brisbane, Queensland, Australia. Doherty earned his bachelor's and master's degrees in veterinary science from the University of Queensland in 1962 and 1966, respectively, and his PhD in pathology from the

University of Edinburgh in Scotland in 1970. Doherty returned to Australia to the John Curtin School of Medical Research within the Australian National University in Canberra, where he collaborated with Rolf M. Zinkernagel on their Nobel Prize–winning research, which described how the immune system recognizes cells infected by viruses.

Peter C. Doherty (1940–)
Source: *Wikimedia Commons,* https://commons.wikimedia. org/wiki/File:Peter_C._ Doherty_2017.jpg

Doherty was at the Wistar Institute in Philadelphia, Pennsylvania from 1975 to 1982, head of the pathology department at the Curtin School in Canberra from

1982 to 1988, and chair of the immunology department at St. Jude Children's Hospital in Memphis, Tennessee, from 1988 to 2001. He later joined the faculty at the University of Melbourne.

Doherty has received many awards, including the Albert Lasker Award for Basic Medical Research in 1995, the Nobel Prize in Physiology or Medicine jointly with Rolf M. Zinkernagel of Switzerland in 1996, and Australian of the Year in 1997. Doherty is the author of six books: *The Beginner's Guide to Winning the Nobel Prize, A Light History of Hot Air, Sentinel Chickens, The Knowledge Wars, Pandemics – What Everyone Needs to Know,* and *Their Fate Is Our Fate – How Birds Foretell Threats to Our Health and Our World.*

Further Reading

- Peter C. Doherty. Accessed Jan 10, 2021. www.britannica.com/biography/Peter-C-Doherty
- Peter C. Doherty. Accessed Jan 10, 2021. www.nobelprize.org/prizes/medicine/1996/doherty
- Prof. Dr. Peter Charles Doherty. Accessed Jan 10, 2021. www.mediatheque.lindau-nobel.org/laureates/doherty

James Law

James Law (1838–1921) was born on February 13, 1838, in Edinburgh, Scotland. He enrolled in the Edinburgh Veterinary College, now the Royal (Dick) School of Veterinary Studies, at age 16, and graduated with honors in 1857. Law was also educated in the medical school at Edinburgh University and received additional training at the veterinary schools in Alfort and Lyon in France.

Law returned to Scotland to work with John Gamgee and in 1860 joined Gamgee's New Veterinary College in Edinburgh where he taught anatomy and materia medica. In 1861, Law was awarded his diploma from and became a member of the Royal College of

James Law (1838–1921)
Photo courtesy of Cornell
University Library

Veterinary Surgeons (RCVS). In 1877, he became a Fellow of the RCVS. In 1865, Gamgee moved the New Veterinary College to London, and Law followed. When the College failed, Law moved to Ireland to practice veterinary medicine.

On the recommendation of John Gamgee, in 1868, Andrew Dickson White, President of Cornell University, recruited Law to serve as Chair of the Department of Veterinary Science. While at Cornell, Law authored a 45-page report on the equine influenza epizootic of 1872. In 1882 and 1883, Law chaired the US Treasury Cattle Commission. Law continued teaching veterinary students until 1896 when the New York State Veterinary College at Cornell University officially opened. In 1906, Law was elected president of the AVMA and served a 2-year term. Called a great teacher of great men, James Law was America's first university veterinary professor who raised the bar for academic standards.

Further Reading

- Murnane TG. James Law: America's first veterinary epidemiologist and the equine influenza epizootic of 1872. *Vet Herit.* 2008;31(2):33–37.

- Nolan RS. James Law: a great teacher of great men. *J Am Vet Med Assoc.* 2013;242(3):286–289.

- Smith DF. James Law, teacher of veterinary medicine. *Perspectives Vet Med.* April 17, 2014.

- Teigen P. Law, Billings, Lyman, Williams and Pearson: five Gilded Age biographies. *Vet Herit.* 2010;33(1):10–16.

- Teigen P. Law, James (1838–1921), veterinarian, educator, and public health advocate. *American National Biography;* 1999.

Alexandre Francois Liautard

Alexandre Liautard (1835–1918) was born in Paris, France. He entered the Veterinary School of Alfort, later transferring to Toulouse, where he graduated circa 1855. After 3 years in the French Army, Liautard immigrated to New York City, where he practiced and also studied medicine at the University Medical College, receiving his medical degree in 1865. In 1857, an act was passed to establish the New York College of Veterinary Surgeons. Liautard's practice was the site of the college, and clinical instruction began in 1864. He later founded the American Veterinary College and became its dean in 1875. These colleges served as the template for veterinary education today.

Alexandre Francois Liautard (1835–1918)
Source: *Am Vet Rev.* 1901 Jul;25:245. *HathiTrust Digital Library*, https://hdl.handle.net/2027/uiuo.ark:/13960/t4km6q423

In 1863, Liautard participated in organizing the US Veterinary Medical Association (now the AVMA) and was elected to serve as the first secretary. He was elected president twice, serving from 1875 to 1877 and from 1886 to 1887, and held official positions until 1900. He was the first editor of the *American Veterinary Review,* now known as the *Journal of the American Veterinary Medical Association.*

Liautard advocated for a national examination for veterinary students before graduation, called for food sanitation laws, and campaigned to have veterinarians fill public health positions. He is recognized as the father of the American veterinary profession.

Further Reading

- Alexandre Liautard (Obituary). *J Am Vet Med Assoc.* 1918;53:296–298.
- Crawford LM. A tribute to Alexandre Liautard, the father of the American veterinary profession. *J Am Vet Med Assoc.* 1976;169:35–37.

• Larkin M. Alexandre Francois Liautard: bringing veterinary medicine to the fore. *J Am Vet Med Assoc.* 2013;242(1):6–10.

Mark L. Morris, Sr.

Mark Loren Morris, Sr. (1900–1993) was born November 18, 1900, in Adams County, Colorado. He earned his veterinary degree from Cornell University in 1926. In 1928, Morris opened the Raritan Hospital for Animals in Edison, New Jersey, one of the few hospitals to focus on companion animals and especially nutrition.

In 1933, Morris was a co-founder and served as the first president of the American Animal Hospital Association. Working with Rutgers University, he

Mark L. Morris, Sr. (1900–1993)
Photo courtesy of the Morris Animal Foundation

developed his first pet food in 1939, the same year he met Morris Frank, national ambassador for the Seeing Eye guide dog program. Frank's guide dog, Buddy, had serious kidney disease, and he was desperate to find a cure for his dog. Morris prescribed nutritional management and when Buddy was fed his new pet food, his health improved. Demand for the new formula, which Morris and his wife made in their kitchen, grew significantly. To make enough supply, Morris negotiated an agreement with Hill Packing Company, Topeka, Kansas. He continued to develop new nutritional formulas for pet foods, which Hill's produced, packaged, and marketed. Morris is known as the founder of Hill's Pet Nutrition.

In 1948, Morris founded the Morris Animal Foundation, the world's largest private supporter of companion animal and wildlife research. Morris served as president of the AVMA from 1961 to 1962. He died on July 8, 1993, leaving his son, Mark Morris, Jr., to carry on his work.

Further Reading

- Burns K. Legends: innovator in nutrition, Dr. Mark L. Morris Sr. developed therapeutic diets for pets. *J Am Vet Med Assoc.* 2013;243(5):602–603.

- Haselbush WC. *Mark Morris: Veterinarian.* R.R. Donnelley & Sons; 1984.

Frederick Douglass Patterson

Frederick Douglass Patterson (1901–1988) was born October 10, 1901, in Washington DC. Both of Patterson's parents died of tuberculosis when he was 2 years old, so he was raised by family members, primarily his sister, Bessie. Bessie enrolled Patterson in a private school, Samuel Huston College in Austin, Texas. Patterson later studied in the Agriculture Department at Prairie View Normal and Industrial Institute (now Prairie View A&M University). He earned his DVM and MS degrees from Iowa State College in 1923 and 1927, respectively. He taught at Virginia State College before joining Tuskegee Normal and Industrial Institute (later Tuskegee Institute, now Tuskegee University) in 1928. In 1932, Patterson earned his PhD degree from Cornell University.

Frederick D. Patterson (1901–1988)
Photo courtesy of the Tuskegee University Archives, Tuskegee University

Patterson was head of the veterinary division at Tuskegee, then the School of Agriculture, and became Tuskegee's third president from 1935 to 1953. In 1944, Patterson founded the School of Veterinary Medicine at Tuskegee Institute.

Patterson was instrumental in obtaining a federal grant to develop Moton Field, where young African Americans learned to fly military aircraft, and, in fact, he was the spark for the legendary Tuskegee Airmen of World War II.

In 1944, Patterson also founded the United Negro College Fund, which has raised over $2 billion for 39 colleges and universities. In 1987, Patterson was awarded the Presidential Medal of Freedom by President Ronald Reagan, the foremost US civilian decoration, awarded to individuals who have made "an especially meritorious contribution to the security or national interests of the United States, world peace, cultural or other significant public or private endeavors." Patterson died on April 26, 1988, in New Rochelle, New York.

Further Reading

- Adams E. *The Legacy: A History of the Tuskegee University School of Veterinary Medicine.* Media Center Press; 1995.
- Frederick Douglass Patterson, 1901-1988. Accessed Jan 10, 2021. www.uncf.org/pages/Frederick-douglass-patterson-2
- Larkin M. Frederick Douglass Patterson: an educational philanthropist. *J Am Vet Med Assoc.* 2013;243(3):316–318.

Daniel E. Salmon

Daniel Elmer Salmon (1850–1914), America's first DVM, was born in Mount Olive, New Jersey, July 23, 1850. Both his parents died by the time he was 8 years old, and he was raised by his cousin. Salmon was in the first class to enter Cornell University in 1868, earning a Bachelor of Veterinary Science degree (under James Law) in 1872 and a DVM degree in 1876, the first doctorate of veterinary medicine awarded in the United States. Salmon's clinical work was completed at the Alfort Veterinary School in France. In 1872, Salmon briefly practiced in Newark, New Jersey, and then Ashville, North Carolina in 1875.

Salmon helped to eliminate contagious pleuropneumonia in New York in 1879 and later joined the US Department of Agriculture (USDA), studying animal diseases, especially Texas fever, in the southern states. In 1883, he was asked to organize a veterinary division within the USDA. This division became the Bureau of Animal Industry, which was under Salmon's leadership for 21 years from 1884 until 1905. During this time, contagious bovine pleuropneumonia was eradicated in the United States and the federal meat inspection program was established.

In 1892, Salmon also founded the National Veterinary College in Washington DC, serving as dean until 1898. He was the last president of the US Veterinary Medical Association, in 1897–1898, which then became the American Veterinary Medical Association. After his years with the USDA, in 1905, Salmon moved to Uruguay to become the founding director of the National Veterinary School in Montevideo until 1912. He then relocated to Montana and pursued laboratory work and helped support ranchers with livestock poisoning incidental to copper mining pollution.

Daniel Elmer Salmon (1850–1914)
Source: Salmon DE. *The United States Bureau of Animal Industry at the Close of the Nineteenth Century.* [Souvenir volume]. Washington: The Author, 1901; p 20.

The bacterial genus *Salmonella* was named after Salmon in 1900. Through the control and eradication of animal diseases and his work in public health, Daniel E. Salmon had a profound impact on veterinary medicine and human health.

Further Reading

• Cima G. Daniel E. Salmon: America's first DVM. *J Am Vet Med Assoc.* 2013;242(5):584–585.

• Daniel Elmer Salmon, B.V.Sc., D.V.M. (Obituary). *Am Vet Rev.* 1914;XLVI:93–95. Accessed Jan 10, 2021, at https://hdl.handle.net/2027/uc1.b3300332

- Koenig KJ. The Bureau of Animal Industry and veterinary professionalism at the turn of the 20th century. *Vet Herit.* 2009;32(1):12–17.
- Quivik FL. The tragic Montana career of Dr. D.E. Salmon. *Montana: The Magazine of Western History.* Spring 2007;32–47.
- Daniel E. Salmon. Special Collections, USDA National Agricultural Library. Accessed Jan 10, 2021. https://www.nal.usda.gov/exhibits/speccoll/exhibits/show/parasitic-diseases-with-econom/item/8203/

Calvin W. Schwabe

Calvin W. Schwabe (1927–2006) was born March 15, 1927, in Newark, New Jersey. He earned a BS degree in biology from Virginia Polytechnic Institute in 1948, an MS degree in zoology from the University of Hawaii in 1950, and a DVM degree from Auburn University in 1954 with highest honors. He also earned an MPH in tropical public health and a PhD in parasitology-tropical public health from Harvard University in 1955 and 1956, respectively.

From 1956 to 1966, Schwabe was a member of the medical and public health faculties of the American University of Beirut, where he founded a joint Department of Tropical Health within the medical and public health faculties and a Department of Epidemiology and Biostatistics within the School of Public Health. In 1960, Schwabe began to serve as a consultant to, and later directing parasitic disease programs for, the World Health Organization. In 1966, Schwabe joined the faculty at the University of California–Davis, School of Veterinary Medicine, where he established the Department of Epidemiology and Preventive Medicine

Calvin W. Schwabe (1927–2006)
Photo courtesy of the UC-Davis School of Veterinary Medicine

(now the Department of Medicine and Epidemiology), the first of its kind in any veterinary school in the world. Schwabe promoted the concept of "One Medicine" that was earlier noted by Rudolph Virchow and William Osler.

Schwabe is considered the father of veterinary epidemiology and a giant within the One Health movement. He died on June 24, 2006.

Further Reading

- Nolan RS. Calvin W. Schwabe: the accidental epidemiologist. *J Am Vet Med Assoc.* 2013;243(1):27–29.
- Schultz MG, Schantz P. Photo Quiz: *Emerg Infect Dis.* 2011;17(12):2365–2367.
- Schwabe CW. *Cattle, Priests, and Progress in Medicine* (The Wesley W. Spink lectures on comparative medicine). University of Minnesota Press; 1978.

Theobald Smith

Theobald Smith (1859–1934) was born in Albany, New York, on July 31, 1859. He earned a Bachelor of Philosophy degree from Cornell University in 1881 and an MD degree from Albany Medical College in 1883. In December 1883, Smith began working as a research assistant under Daniel E. Salmon, then Chief of the Veterinary Division, US Department of Agriculture (USDA). When the Bureau of Animal Industry was formed within the USDA in 1884, Smith became an Inspector and continued in that position until 1895. During his first 2 years at the Bureau, Smith discovered a new species of bacteria (*Salmonella enterica,* formerly called *Salmonella choleraesuis*), which he thought was the cause of hog cholera. The genus was named after Daniel Salmon.

In 1888, Smith turned his attention to Texas fever, a debilitating cattle disease and, along with veterinarians Cooper Curtice and Fred L. Kilbourne, discovered the responsible tick-borne protozoan parasite, *Babesia bigemina*. This marked the first time that an arthropod was linked with the transmission of an infectious disease and enabled the discovery of insects as vectors in diseases such as yellow fever, plague, and malaria. About a decade later, Smith demonstrated the subtle differences of the avian, bovine, and human tubercle bacilli and, in opposition to Robert Koch, showed they presented risk of human transmission, particularly from unpasteurized milk.

Theobald Smith (1859–1934)
Source: *Wikimedia Commons,* https://commons.wikimedia.org/wiki/File:Theobald_Smith.jpg

Smith taught at The Columbian University, Washington DC (now George Washington University), from 1886 to 1895, establishing the school's Department of Bacteriology. In 1895, he moved to Harvard University to serve as professor of comparative pathology and to direct the pathology laboratory at the Massachusetts State Board of Health. In 1915, Smith joined the Rockefeller Institute for Medical Research in New York City as director of the department of animal pathology, where he remained until his retirement in 1929.

In 1933, Smith was awarded the Royal Society's prestigious Copley Gold Medal "For his original research and observation on diseases of animals and man." Theobald Smith died December 10, 1934, in New York City.

Further Reading

- Burns K. Theobald Smith: a pioneer in research. *J Am Vet Med Assoc.* 2013;242(9):1192–1193.

- Rosenkrantz BG. The trouble with bovine tuberculosis. *Bull Hist Med.* 1985;59(2):155–175.

- Schultz M. Theobald Smith. *Emerg Infect Dis.* 2008;14(12):1940–1942.

James H. Steele

James Harlan Steele (1913–2013) was born on April 3, 1913, in Chicago, Illinois. Steele earned his DVM degree at Michigan State College in 1941 and his MPH degree at Harvard University in 1945. Cecil Drinker, Dean of the School of Public Health at Harvard, encouraged Steele to launch the veterinary public health program in the US Public Health Service, which he did in Washington DC in 1945. Two years later, Steele moved to Atlanta and organized the veterinary division within the Centers for Disease Control and Prevention.

James H. Steele (1913–2013)
Source: *Wikimedia Commons*, https://commons.wikimedia. org/wiki/File:James_H_Steele_ CDC_IM-2003-F1.jpg

In 1950, Steele founded the American Board of Veterinary Public Health, now known as the American College of Veterinary Preventive Medicine. In 1968, he became the first Assistant Surgeon General for Veterinary Affairs in the US Public Health Service, and in 1970 he became the Deputy Assistant Secretary for Health and Human Services. In 1971, after retiring from the Centers for Disease Control, Steele was appointed Professor of Environmental Health at the University of Texas School of Public Health. He also became Editor-in-Chief of the first comprehensive series of medical texts in the world on zoonotic diseases, the *CRC Handbook Series in Zoonoses*.

James Steele is known as the father of veterinary public health and promoted the One Health concept throughout his career. He died at age 100 on November 10, 2013.

Further Reading

- Carter CN, Hoobler CG. *Animal Health, Human Health, One Health: The Life and Legacy of Dr. James H. Steele.* Distrib. by the University of Texas School of Public Health; 2009.
- Currier RW. In memoriam: James Harlan Steele, 3 April 1913 – 10 November 2013. *Vet Herit.* 2014;37(1):38–40.
- Pincock S. James Harlan Steele. *Lancet.* 2014;383(9913):212.
- White MJ. James Harlan Steele: the father of veterinary public health. *J Am Vet Med Assoc.* 2013;242(7):894–897.

James A. Wight

James Alfred Wight (1916–1995), known by the pen name James Herriot, was born on October 3, 1916, in Sunderland, County Durham, England. The family moved to Glasgow, Scotland, and Wight entered the Glasgow Veterinary College, qualifying in 1939. Wight returned to Sunderland to practice but soon moved to Thirsk in Yorkshire. Wight practiced here for the rest of his life except for serving in the Royal Air Force during World War II.

Wight entertained millions of readers with stories of his life in Yorkshire, England, as a country veterinarian, caring for both his animal patients and their sometimes eccentric owners. Although he collected information for many years, he did not start writing until age 50. His stories were published under the name James Herriot in *If Only They Could Talk* in 1970 and *It Shouldn't Happen*

James Alf Wight, aka James Herriot (1916–1995)
Photo courtesy of the World of James Herriot Museum, Thirsk, North Yorkshire, England

to a Vet in 1972. These were subsequently published in the United States as *All Creatures Great and Small,* resulting in a series of popular books, films, and a PBS British television series of the same name.

Wight borrowed the pen name James Herriot from a Bristol City soccer goalkeeper who played for teams in Scotland, England, and South Africa. More than 60 million of Wight's books have been sold and translated into more than 20 languages. Wight was named an honorary fellow of the Royal College of Veterinary Surgeons. His other accolades include the Literary Prize from the University of Edinburgh, Order of the British Empire, the AVMA Award of Appreciation, and the British Veterinary Association's first Chiron Award. After Wight died in 1995, the library at Glasgow Veterinary College was dedicated in his memory. Wight was a gifted storyteller, and his veterinary experiences told with kindness, compassion, and often amusement, have influenced many young people to become veterinarians.

Further Reading

• Cima G. Modest veterinarian, beloved author: Dr. James A. Wight's experience in barns and homes reached millions. *J Am Vet Med Assoc.* 2011;239(1):32–33.

• Luebering JE. James Herriot: British veterinarian and writer. *Encyclopedia Britannica.* Feb 19, 2020. Accessed Jan 10, 2021. www.britannica.com/biography/James-Herriot

THE PRINCIPLES OF VETERINARY MEDICAL ETHICS

Veterinarians practice veterinary medicine in a variety of situations and circumstances. Exemplary professional conduct upholds the dignity of the veterinary profession. All veterinarians are expected to adhere to a progressive code of ethical conduct known as the Principles of Veterinary Medical Ethics.

1. A veterinarian shall be influenced only by the welfare of the patient, the needs of the client, the safety of the public, and the need to uphold the public trust vested in the veterinary profession, and shall avoid conflicts of interest or the appearance thereof.

2. A veterinarian shall provide competent veterinary medical clinical care under the terms of a veterinarian-client-patient relationship, with compassion and respect for animal welfare and human health.

3. A veterinarian shall uphold the standards of professionalism, be honest in all professional interactions, and report veterinarians who are deficient in character or competence to the appropriate entities.

4. A veterinarian shall respect the law and also recognize a responsibility to seek changes to laws and regulations which are contrary to the best interests of the patient and public health.

5. A veterinarian shall respect the rights of clients, colleagues, and other health professionals, and shall safeguard medical information within the confines of the law.

6. A veterinarian shall continue to study, apply, and advance scientific knowledge, maintain a commitment to veterinary medical education, make relevant information available to clients, colleagues, the public, and obtain consultation or referral when indicated.

7. A veterinarian shall, in the provision of appropriate patient care, except in emergencies, be free to choose whom to serve, with whom to associate, and the environment in which to provide veterinary medical care.

8. A veterinarian shall recognize a responsibility to participate in activities contributing to the improvement of the community and the betterment of public health.

9. A veterinarian should view, evaluate, and treat all persons in any professional activity or circumstance in which they may be involved, solely as individuals on the basis of their own personal abilities, qualifications, and other relevant characteristics.

Source: https://www.avma.org/resources-tools/avma-policies/principles-veterinary-medical-ethics-avma